BFI Film Classics

The BFI Film Classics series introduces, interprets and celebrates landmarks of world cinema. Each volume offers an argument for the film's 'classic' status, together with discussion of its production and reception history, its place within a genre or national cinema, an account of its technical and aesthetic importance, and in many cases, the author's personal response to the film.

For a full list of titles in the series, please visit https://www.bloomsbury.com/uk/series/bfi-film-classics/

Photo by Universal History Archive/UIG via Getty Images

Sunset Boulevard

Steven Cohan

BFI

THE BRITISH FILM INSTITUTE
Bloomsbury Publishing Plc, 50 Bedford Square, London, WC1B 3DP, UK
Bloomsbury Publishing Inc, 1385 Broadway, New York, NY 10018, USA
Bloomsbury Publishing Ireland, 29 Earlsfort Terrace, Dublin 2, D02 AY28, Ireland

First published in Great Britain by Bloomsbury in 2022
Reprinted in 2024, 2025
on behalf of the
British Film Institute
21 Stephen Street, London W1T 1LN
www.bfi.org.uk

The BFI is the lead organisation for film in the UK and the distributor of Lottery funds for film. Our mission is to ensure that film is central to our cultural life, in particular by supporting and nurturing the next generation of filmmakers and audiences. We serve a public role which covers the cultural, creative and economic aspects of film in the UK.

Cover artwork: © Rania Moudarres
Series cover design: Louise Dugdale
Series text design: Ketchup/SE14
Images from *Sunset Boulevard* (Billy Wilder, 1950), © Paramount Pictures; *One, Two, Three* (Billy Wilder, 1961), © The Mirisch Company/Pyramid Productions; *Fedora* (Billy Wilder, 1978), Geria Film/Bavaria Atelier GmbH/Société Française de Production

A catalogue record for this book is available from the British Library.

A catalog record for this book is available from the Library of Congress.

ISBN: PB: 978-1-8390-2408-5
ePDF: 978-1-8390-2410-8
ePUB: 978-1-8390-2409-2

Produced for Bloomsbury Publishing Plc by Sophie Contento
Printed and bound in Great Britain

For product safety related questions contact productsafety@bloomsbury.com.

Contents

Acknowledgments

I wish to thank the anonymous readers for their enthusiasm for and support of this book at the proposal and manuscript stages; Sophie Contento for the care with which she prepared the book for publication; and my long-time editor and friend, Rebecca Barden, for inviting me to propose a volume for this series.

I dedicate this book to Andrea, Matt, Roger and Will: thank you for your friendship.

But *Sunset Boulevard*, as I look back at it, was a miraculous series of lucky incidents that helped the picture. I wanted DeMille and I got DeMille. I wanted somebody who at one time had directed a picture with Swanson and I found Stroheim. And I got to use the picture *Queen Kelly*. And I needed the Paramount studio, I got the Paramount studio. Whatever I needed. I was very, very lucky.

Billy Wilder[1]

1 'A Most Unusual Motion Picture'

All right, Mr DeMille. I'm ready for my close-up.

I *am* big! It's the pictures that got small.

Narrated in voiceover by a corpse floating face down in a swimming pool, Billy Wilder's *Sunset Boulevard* (1950) is, as Paramount's advertising declared at the time, 'a most unusual motion picture'.[2] The ghostly voice of Joe Gillis (William Holden) focuses most of the narrative with his voiceover commentary, as he promises at the start to reveal 'the facts, the whole truth' about his own death, because 'an old-time star is involved. One of the biggest.'

Following the opening credits, with the film's title represented by a shot of the street name stencilled on a kerb, *Sunset Boulevard*

shows police cars careening to a mansion and shots of a young man's body floating in the swimming pool as the homicide squad inspects and photographs it; but the story proper begins six months earlier, with Joe, an out-of-work and broke screenwriter who owes back rent on his tiny apartment and three months' payment on his automobile, trying to elude the two repo men who have come to collect the vehicle. He goes to Paramount to pitch a baseball script, 'Bases Loaded', to producer Sheldrake (Fred Clark) but reader Betty Schaefer (Nancy Olson) dismisses it out of hand as 'just a rehash of something that wasn't very good to begin with'. Joe then tries calling friends and 'yes-men' at various studios around town, again to no avail, and he fights with his agent, who tells him to find new management. Joe is driving on Sunset when the repo men catch sight of his car and a chase ensues, until Joe gets a blowout and pulls into the hidden driveway of a large, imposing mansion that looks old, unkempt and deserted. 'A great big white elephant of a place,' he describes it in voiceover. 'The kind crazy movie people built in the crazy twenties. A neglected house gets an unhappy look. This one had it in spades.'

This neglected, unhappy house belongs to silent screen star Norma Desmond (Gloria Swanson). Her career ended with the arrival of sound two decades earlier and now she lives alone with just one servant, her butler Max Von Mayerling (Erich von Stroheim). They mistake Joe for an undertaker who is due to arrive for the burial of Norma's deceased pet chimpanzee. When Norma learns that Joe is a screenwriter she wants him to look at 'Salome', a massive script she has written for her 'return' to the screen (not a 'comeback', a word she detests). Joe thinks that, just as he has outwitted the repo men by hiding his car, he can take advantage of Norma and earn a lot of money working with her on the script. 'I felt kind of pleased with the way I handled the situation,' he comments in voiceover.

But it soon turns out that Norma handles Joe more skilfully. Before he agrees to stay she has had Max prepare the room over the garage for him to spend the night. When Joe wakes the next morning he discovers that Max has also paid the back rent and moved all his things there; later, when it rains and the ceiling leaks, Max moves him into 'the husband's room' in the main house. Norma lets the

repo men take away his car, removing his independence. She buys him expensive clothes and gives him jewellery; but the only cash he ends up getting is some loose change she wins at her bridge games with what he calls 'the waxworks' – Buster Keaton, H. B. Warner and Anna Q. Nilsson. On New Year's Eve, Norma confesses that she is madly in love with Joe, and he flees from her declaration, hoping to take refuge at his friend Artie Green's (Jack Webb) place.

Artie is an assistant director hosting a New Year's Eve party with a large crowd of Hollywood's below-the-line labourers and bit players. There Joe runs into Artie's fiancée, who, as it happens, is Betty Schaefer. Feeling guilty for her harsh dismissal of 'Bases Loaded' in Sheldrake's office, she has found in 'Dark Windows', one of Joe's older stories, a six-page flashback that she thinks has the potential to expand into something good. The two engage in good-natured repartee until Joe learns that Norma has attempted suicide following his rejection of her earlier that evening. His guilt prompts a return to Sunset Boulevard, where he willingly becomes Norma's gigolo lover in earnest.

Now *Sunset Boulevard* balances two intersecting plots about ambitious people on the margins of Hollywood. Norma has Max deliver her script of 'Salome' to the famous real-life director Cecil B. DeMille, with whom she had made many silent pictures. When she gets a call from Gordon Cole at Paramount, she assumes he is a DeMille underling; after waiting for the director himself to call, she finally pays a visit to DeMille at the studio, where he is directing *Samson and Delilah* (1949). Cole only wanted to borrow for another movie Norma's expensive, hand-crafted foreign car, an Isotta-Fraschini, but she thinks DeMille plans to do 'Salome' with her starring. When Norma arrives at the soundstage the people working there remember her and cluster around in adoration.

Meanwhile, Joe, who by this time has settled into his role as Norma's younger kept man, sees Betty walking to her cubicle on the lot and follows her there. He still refuses to collaborate with her on a script but soon succumbs to the temptation and, with Artie away on location and the studio deserted nights, the two work together in Betty's tiny office on an untitled love story based on the 'Dark Windows' flashback. Each evening Joe takes the Isotta-Fraschini to the Paramount lot once Norma, fatigued from the rigorous beauty regimen she undergoes to prepare for her anticipated return to the screen, falls asleep, or so he thinks. As they work on their script, enjoying their collaboration, Betty and Joe fall in love and he believes that he may be able to keep her from learning about his relationship with Norma; but the jealous older woman has become aware of his night-time disappearances and finds in Joe's coat pocket the typescript of his and Betty's script. She telephones Betty to make her wonder about where, how and with whom Joe lives, hoping to scare off her rival. Joe intercepts this call and tells Betty to come to Norma's mansion on Sunset Boulevard in order to see for herself.

Joe decides to do the noble thing. He confesses the truth about his relationship with Norma to Betty, who refuses to listen and orders him to leave with her immediately. After sending her back to Artie by pretending that he enjoys the benefits of being kept by a wealthy older woman, Joe packs the clothes he had when he first arrived, intending to return to his hometown of Dayton, Ohio, and his old job on the local newspaper. Hysterical and becoming crazed, Norma begs Joe to stay, declaring she will shoot herself if he leaves her. He refuses to give her threat credence but tells her the truth: that Max has been writing the numerous fan letters she has been getting all these years, and that DeMille was too kind-hearted to tell her that Paramount only wanted her car and has no intention of making 'Salome'. These revelations cause her final breakdown. 'No one ever leaves a star,' Norma whispers. 'That's what makes one a star.' Joe leaves despite her pleas and she shoots him twice in the back and once, when he turns around, in the stomach. His lifeless body falls into the swimming pool.

Joe's death returns us to the film's opening scene, with the police, reporters, gossip columnist Hedda Hopper and newsreel men clustered around Norma, now lost in a fantasy world. 'The dream she had clung to so desperately had enfolded her,' the ghostly Joe intones. To get her to leave with them, the police encourage her to think the person shooting newsreel footage is DeMille's cameraman and that Max, positioned near him, is DeMille. As she makes her way down the staircase, writhing sensuously in character as the temptress Salome, she stops short because she is 'too happy' to continue, so delighted to be back at work. 'You see, this is my life. It always will be. There's nothing else – just us and the cameras and those wonderful people out there in the dark.' Declaring she is now ready for her close-up, Norma moves towards the camera, her close-up blurring as a dissolve to the end title card and cast list.

Sunset Boulevard had its world premiere on 10 August 1950 at Radio City Music Hall in New York City, where it had a highly profitable seven-week run according to *Variety*. The following week it began a successful engagement at the Carlton cinema in London's West End, and a week after that it opened at the two Paramount theatres in Los Angeles before rolling out to other major cities during September and October. Initially, the film did very well at the box office – at least until it went to smaller theatres 'in the sticks', as

Variety put it, where it met a more lacklustre reception 'in a number of minor openings' ('"Sunset" Looks to Music Hall Record' 1950). In his favourable review James Agee mused that 'this is essentially a picture-maker's picture. I very much enjoy and respect it, but it seems significant to me that among other interested amateurs there is a wide difference of reaction, ranging from moderate liking or disappointment all the way to boredom, intense dislike, or even contempt' (1950: 283). Nonetheless, in *Variety*'s listing of the ninety top-grossing films of 1950 in the US and Canada, *Sunset Boulevard* placed twenty-ninth with $2,300,000 in rentals, the amount returned to Paramount from theatres ('Top Grossers' 1951).

From the start, *Sunset Boulevard* was well received by critics and people in the industry, for whom invitation-only previews had become a hot ticket prior to its theatrical openings. As Edwin

Los Angeles Times, 20 August 1950, Part IV, p. 3

HIT PICTURE TO CONTINUE

"Sunset Boulevard," unusual Hollywood film story which has racked up box-office records in every situation, continues at the Paramount, Hollywood and Downtown Theaters, moving into a fourth week today.

The subject, tailor made for Gloria Swanson's return to the screen, costars her with William Holden and Erich von Stroheim. It is a penetrating study of yesterday's Hollywood and today's film industry told in terms of a faded screen star's attempts at a comeback.

Los Angeles Times, 14 September 1950, p. 65

Schallert (1950) noted in his *Los Angeles Times* review, '"Sunset Boulevard" arrives well heralded in advance, and its excellence is fast becoming a legend.' The praise culminated in eleven Academy Award nominations, including ones for Best Picture, for each of its main performers – William Holden, Gloria Swanson, Erich von Stroheim and Nancy Olson – and for Wilder's direction and his collaboration with D. M. Marshman Jr and producer Charles Brackett on the screenplay. At the ceremony in April 1951 it won three: for the writing, Franz Waxman's music score and the black-and-white art and set decoration.

Today, *Sunset Boulevard* remains unforgettable as well as unusual. It is considered a prime example of film noir and its story of Hollywood is still one of the darkest and one of the best. Its many quotable lines of dialogue have entered popular culture's lexicon. The two most famous ones, quoted at the start of this chapter, were ranked seventh and twenty-fourth in the American Film Institute's 100 favourite movie quotes. *Sunset Boulevard* entered the National Film Registry of the Library of Congress in 1989 and the American Film Institute placed it sixteenth among the Greatest Movies of All Time. Its influence has been significant, too; subsequent films about the motion picture industry, such as Robert Altman's *The Player* (1992) and David Lynch's *Mulholland Drive* (2001), have evoked or alluded to *Sunset Boulevard*, and the references speak to a knowing

The main cast of *Sunset Boulevard*: William Holden (Joe Gillis), Gloria Swanson (Norma Desmond), Nancy Olson (Betty Schaefer) and Erich von Stroheim (Max Von Mayerling)

audience of film aficionados. Similarly, *Sunset Boulevard* has been affectionally parodied on television, most notably several times in a recurring sketch on *The Carol Burnett Show* (CBS, 1967–78); and it became a successful stage musical, opening in London and Los Angeles in 1993 and on Broadway the following year.

Clearly, the enduring fame of *Sunset Boulevard* has lasted well beyond its theatrical release in 1950. Everyone now recognises that Billy Wilder's film is a classic, a product of its own historical moment, yet one which has continued to intrigue as well as entertain scholars, fans and film-makers since its release seven decades ago.

2 Making *Sunset Boulevard*

Sunset Boulevard was the final collaboration of Billy Wilder and Charles Brackett.[3] They had worked together at Paramount since 1936 as a screenwriting team with a number of commercial and critical successes, notably *Bluebeard's Eighth Wife* (1938), *Midnight* (1939), *Arise, My Love* (1940) and *Hold Back the Dawn* (1941). Additionally, the duo wrote *Ninotchka* (1939) on loan to MGM and *Ball of Fire* (1941) for independent producer Samuel Goldwyn and RKO. Although he always thought of himself first and foremost as a writer, Wilder says he turned to directing his scripts after Mitchell Leisen cut an important scene from *Hold Back the Dawn* to appease star Charles Boyer, who refused to play it. Thus began a string of hits for Wilder as a director that lasted through to the end of the decade, most but not all written with Brackett: *The Major and the Minor* (1942), *Five Graves to Cairo* (1943), *Double Indemnity* (1944, written with Raymond Chandler), *The Lost Weekend* (1945) and *A Foreign Affair* (1948). The only disappointment was a Bing Crosby musical, *The Emperor's Waltz* (1948). Brackett eventually produced their films, as well as several without Wilder, such as *The Uninvited* (1944) and *To Each His Own* (1946), both successes.

'These collaborators', the *New York Times* reported in 1948, 'exercise an astonishing degree of self-government on the Paramount lot' and their 'setup is as rare as radium' for Hollywood (Koury 1948). Although Wilder states in that same article that 'he and Brackett are "the happiest couple in Hollywood"', that was not quite the case. By all accounts the two men made a feisty and quarrelsome pair who yet complemented each other's talents. As the *Times* writer pointed out, Brackett's 'refined literary tastes' stabilised Wilder's 'high intellectual wattage'.

Billy Wilder

Charles Brackett

They came from vastly different backgrounds. Wilder was born in what was then a Polish province of Austria, lived with his family in Vienna until he finished high school when he moved on his own to Berlin in 1926. There he worked as a journalist and scriptwriter. As 'Billie' Wilder he co-wrote a silent film, *People on Sunday* (1930), collaborating with other novice film-makers who, as refugees from the Nazis, would also become important to Hollywood as future directors: Fred Zinnemann, Robert Siodmak and Edgar G. Ulmer. With the Nazi threat increasingly evident, the Jewish Wilder migrated to Paris in 1933, where he directed a feature film, *Mauvaise graine* (1934). In January 1934 he immigrated to the United States and became a citizen in 1939. An older brother had arrived in the US several years earlier, but the rest of Wilder's family – his mother, stepfather and grandmother – perished in the Holocaust. Once in the US he learned English from the radio, popular music and comic strips.

Brackett, fourteen years Wilder's senior and a World War I veteran, came from an affluent family in New York state. He initially trained in law at Harvard to follow in the footsteps of his father, who was a politician as well as an attorney, but was uninterested in the family profession. Brackett instead wrote novels and published short stories in leading magazines and was hired as a drama critic for the *New Yorker* before travelling to Hollywood in 1932 to work at RKO. It was not a happy situation for him and he returned East, only to be called back to the West Coast with a Paramount contract in 1934. Brackett was active in industry politics, serving as president of the Screenwriters Guild in 1938–9 and on the Executive Board of the Academy of Motion Picture Arts and Sciences during the 1940s, rising to president from 1949 to 1955.

For fifteen years Wilder and Brackett worked together in their three-room office suite on the Paramount lot, 'noted for its informality and conviviality' (Koury 1948). At lunchtime they ate at Lucey's, a restaurant across the street from Paramount, or in the studio's commissary, after which they played The Word Game with others at the writers' table.[4] Afternoons, they napped or played games of cribbage or bridge, and then resumed writing until supper time. Some evenings they continued working at Wilder's home. Hitting their stride quickly with their initial screenplays, they were known by many in Hollywood as a single entity, 'brackettandwilder' (Barnett 1944: 102). As the *New York Times* noted in its profile of the team, Brackett was a composed presence as they worked, while Wilder was a whirling dervish, often wielding a cane to gesticulate what he said while his partner lay reclining on a sofa, scribbling on a yellow writing pad. Remarking about his partner in his diary, Brackett noted, 'Billy Wilder, who paces constantly, has overextravagant ideas, but is stimulating. ... He has humor – a kind of humor that sparks with mine' (Slide 2015: 86).

The men's different temperaments resulted in friction as well as frisson. They knew intimate details about each other's private lives, and both shared a loving friendship with Ernst Lubitsch, the famed director for whom they wrote *Bluebeard's Eighth Wife* and *Ninotchka*, but they rarely socialised together. Whereas Wilder was a sportsman and physically active, Brackett was sedentary and lethargic. Whereas Wilder was a long-time collector of twentieth-century art, Brackett loved gossip and frequently lunched at Perino's with his friend Ruth Waterbury of *Photoplay* magazine. Whereas Wilder was Jewish and a liberal Democrat, Brackett was Protestant and a conservative Republican. Whereas Wilder spoke his mind, had a temper and insulted people easily, Brackett was quieter, more refined in his demeanour and conciliatory – although his diary shows he often took umbrage at cruel or vulgar things his writing partner said to him. It was an open question as to which of the two men was the more chronic hypochondriac. Brackett's grandson, Jim Moore, recalls that the two men 'loved each other, hated each other, defended each other, sold each other out, delighted in the partnership, and longed for the pairing to die' (Slide 2015: xvi–xvii).

On 26 March 1949, the day before shooting began with the first location footage for *Sunset Boulevard* and with the script still unfinished, Brackett mentions in his diary that this is to be his last film with Wilder (Slide 2015: 326). Wilder's biographer, Ed Sikov, reports that when each man had signed new contracts with Paramount in the autumn of 1948 they had 'specified independence from each other' after *Sunset Boulevard* (1998: 305). Yet Brackett noted that he was taken aback when he learned of Wilder's new contractual independence; and in 1960 Brackett told Garson Kanin that he had not seen Wilder's 'shattering' announcement about a split coming (306). Joseph McBride, however, calls Brackett's professed shock 'a sign of self-delusion', since he frequently wrote in his diary that he wanted to be free of Wilder (2021: 189). Even though their partnership was ending they continued to work on *Sunset Boulevard* as a team, finishing the screenplay with their co-writer, D. M. 'Mac' Marshman Jr, formerly a reporter for *Life*, and going over the rushes together. Their collaboration continued through two periods of sneak previews and subsequent reshoots of certain scenes that took them to early January 1950. Then the two men went their separate ways professionally.

Who first came up with the idea for *Sunset Boulevard* is unclear. At some point in 1939 or 1940 Wilder wrote on a scrap of paper: 'Silent picture star commits murder. When they arrest her she sees the newsreel cameras and thinks she is back in the movies' (Sikov 1998: 289). It is not evident if or when Wilder showed this note to his partner, or when he himself recalled it. In 1976 he attributed 'the idea of doing a picture with a Hollywood background' to Brackett (American Film Institute [1976] 2001: 27). The first mention of a possible Hollywood picture in Brackett's diary occurred on 18 October 1946 when he and Wilder 'decided that a picture about Hollywood would be the thing which would interest most' (Slide 2015: 295). At the time, Brackett wanted to make a comedy about a silent screen star, and this approach shaped his and Wilder's initial thinking about their Hollywood picture.

By August 1948 Wilder, Brackett and Marshman were working on the project in earnest. They agreed their Hollywood story would be 'all centered around a swimming pool owned by an old silent days' star', but 'nothing about it [is] set as yet' (Slide 2015: 346). A few days later they had one character for the picture and chose a nonsensical title, 'A Can of Beans', as a means of keeping the studio in the dark about their script's Hollywood premise. 'The character is the harassed head of the studio,' Brackett recorded, 'half heavy, half hero, who dies of heart exhaustion driving back from a preview in Pomona. We've also pretty well set on the raddled old picture star who is keeping a young man, probably a writer' (348). The following week, Wilder had found 'a new slant on our Hollywood picture. Mae West as the faded glamor item; Millard Mitchell as her manager; Wally Beery as a Texas oil man who finances her. Funny but infinitely less true than the former set-up' (347–8). The next day, however, the writers 'agreed that the Mae West story, while offering riotous possibilities, could not possibly result in a picture of distinction and began thinking more about the Gloria Swanson set up' (348). This is the first time Brackett mentioned Swanson in conjunction with the new picture, although she had not yet been cast, and Wilder and Brackett had other former screen stars in mind for their main character. Nonetheless, they continued to use 'Swanson' for the as-yet unnamed character in their conversations, and 'Clift' – as in Montgomery Clift, the young male star of *Red River* (1948), who had been cast in the part – for the character that would become Joe Gillis.

At the end of August Wilder came up with the events that lead to Clift hiding his car from the repo men and then encountering Swanson at her house. In early September Wilder devised an opening scene in the county morgue that would later cause problems after the initial sneak previews, and by mid-month, 'another character [was] creeping into the script, a former husband of Swanson's' (Slide 2015: 350). Nonetheless, as September neared its close Brackett worried that they still did not have the storyline ironed out. Marshman had proposed that the star get sexually involved with the younger man, and Wilder decided that she would then kill him (Sikov 1998: 289). This led to Clift's dilemma, which would motivate the story's climax. 'The log jam of our story gave some signs of breaking,' Brackett wrote in his diary. 'Billy, though, saying he detests a Camille scene as corny, is definitely set on a Camille scene for our hero and the pattern now will be: fly caught in spider web, escapes because he falls in love with another fly. To promote the second fly's happiness goes back into the spider web briefly and is killed by the spider … How grisly it sounds, stated like that, but I think the pattern is sound' (Slide 2015: 352; ellipses in original). This development then led to 'Billy's new "thesis": that escape from Gloria's house should be impossible to Clift, not by physical obstruction but by its moral equivalent. The more I consider this the more nonsensical I think it is,' Brackett wrote in his diary (352).

Now they were scouting locations while finessing the meeting of Clift and Swanson in the script. Clift was wavering, claiming he feared the part of the writer was too passive. Wilder persuaded him it wasn't, but Brackett and Marshman did not think Clift was convinced. Although they were still calling the silent star character 'Swanson', neither Brackett nor Wilder thought of her immediately.

They met with Mae West, who refused to act the part of a has-been (and anyway, they had moved far from the comedy of their initial planning); with Mary Pickford at Picfair, who declined (they were thankful afterwards and relieved that she did so); and with Pola Negri on the telephone (they refrained from offering her the role when they heard her thick accent). Other actresses reportedly contacted were Greta Garbo and Norma Shearer, but neither showed interest in the project. By the end of 1948 a partial script was mimeographed. The Clift character was called 'Dan Gillis' and the silent screen star 'Norma Desmond'. The latter name may have been a composite of silent stars Mable Normand and Norma Talmadge, as well as William Desmond Taylor, the director whose notorious murder in 1922 was never solved. And George Cukor suggested to Wilder and Brackett that Norma should be played by Gloria Swanson.

As 1949 began, the writers were still dealing 'with the problem of Gillis changing the position from one of secretary to one of actual lover'. Brackett remained unconvinced about Wilder's decision 'that the motif of writing a screenplay for Desmond should be set in the first scene between her and Gillis' (Slide 2015: 359). Brackett's reluctance to agree with Wilder's choices, all of which were on the mark as the finished product would confirm, set the tone of their fractured collaboration from then on. As writing progressed, they argued about the degree of Norma's sanity, since Brackett felt they were making her appear too insane from the get-go so that 'our boy is kept not by a rich egocentric woman but by a madwoman. That he becomes not only kept but the keeper. Billy defended her sanity stoutly' (367). From the writing of the script, to the filming, to the editing, to the cycles of previews and to the many reshoots, the two men would argue about Norma's mental state – whether to keep her arrogance or add an undercurrent of vulnerability, whether to make her lose her sanity or be crazy from the start.

In his many print and video interviews, Wilder expressed the importance of story structure, and he was known as a skilled constructionist; furthermore, although always uncertain about his command of English and reliant on a co-writer, he had a fine ear for and love of American slang. Brackett and Wilder had brought in Marshman to help them work out the narrative line of *Sunset Boulevard*. 'If', Sikov believes, 'Paramount's accounting figures bear any relation to the work performed, the actual composition of the screenplay for *Sunset Boulevard* was done almost entirely by Marshman and Wilder' (1998: 289). While Brackett's salary in the accounting was for producing, his diary shows that he was an active participant in the writing, even if he functioned mainly as sounding board, scribe and editor as Wilder and Marshman tossed out ideas to resolve the film's third act. Moreover, Brackett's sharp eye for nuance in characterisation and when watching rushes proved invaluable.

Before filming began, having temporarily appeased Clift yet again, they finally met with Gloria Swanson, who arrived from New York City in February for a screen test. Swanson had been one of the biggest stars of the silent era, known for her glamour and lavish lifestyle, her many husbands (including actor Wallace Beery and Henri, the Marquis de la Falaise) and her business acumen, not to mention her skill before the camera. Swanson, Wilder recalled, 'was a star who used to ride in a sedan chair from her dressing room to the set. When she married the Marquis de la Somebody, people were strewing rose petals on the tracks in front of her. She's been one of the all-time great stars, but when she returned to do *Sunset*, she worked like a horse, a Lipizzaner. Swanson got $150,000 to do *Sunset*, one of the great bargains in film history' (Chandler 2002: 146).[5] At the time, Swanson was hosting a television programme in New York City – and television may have been on the writers' minds when Norma declares that the pictures have 'got small'. Asked to do a screen test, Swanson was at first insulted, given all the films she had made for Paramount in her heyday, and anxious because she had always been terrible in tests, so she sought advice from Cukor. He told her, since it was for Brackett and Wilder, 'if they ask you to do ten screen tests, do them, or I will personally shoot you' (Swanson 1980: 479).

Billy Wilder and Gloria Swanson

Swanson added nuance to Norma's characterisation. For instance, in discussing the part with Brackett she argued that, since Norma had a million dollars, real estate downtown and oil wells in Bakersfield, she should not, as the script then described, live in squalor, and this advice was taken (Slide 2015: 362). Similarly,

Swanson agreed to have her collection of photographs adorn the set of Norma's house. Certain real-life factors were worked into the script, such as DeMille's habit of calling her 'young fella' in the past when they had worked together on half a dozen silent films. Swanson, who had her own successful clothing line based in New York, worked closely with Paramount's chief designer Edith Head on Norma's costuming; since the character was a throwback to an earlier era but a wealthy woman conscious of her looks, they came up with clothes that combined Jazz Age materials with Dior's trendy New Look styling (Sikov 1998: 292). Because Norma was 'lost in her own imagination', Head recalled, 'I tried to make her look as if she was always impersonating someone' (Staggs 2002: 119). Yet Head found that Swanson 'had so many costumes already in her mind', and that 'she was recreating a past that she knew and I didn't', which was tremendously helpful (129). Perhaps most important, Swanson kept pressing Wilder and Brackett to make Norma more vulnerable.

Erich von Stroheim was inspired casting, too, because his history with Swanson on their unfinished film *Queen Kelly* provided a valuable subtext for the character of Norma's butler. Stroheim had come to Hollywood from Austria in 1914, where he initially worked as an actor but turned to writing and directing, with a number of important silent films to his credit, in some of which he also performed. His most remembered film is probably *Greed* (1924), based on Frank Norris's novel *McTeague*. He delivered an eight-hour film to MGM, and the studio kept cutting the forty-two reels until it had a more conventional running time. Writing in 1929 for *Der Querschnitt*, the young Billy Wilder began a column on Stroheim by wryly noting that in Hollywood he is simply called 'Von', pronounced 'one'. 'And if a Hollywood greenhorn should ask, "Why do you call Stroheim 'one'?" – the answer is: because every company can shoot only one film with him, then it goes broke' (Wilder 2021: 148).

According to Sam Staggs, Stroheim 'possessed the most lurid imagination in silent Hollywood. Not many moviemakers have topped him to this day' (2002: 256–7). Swanson had hired Stroheim to direct her in *Queen Kelly*, which her then-lover Joseph Kennedy financed. A silent film made at the same time that the industry was discovering sound, this was to be a tale of a convent girl (Swanson) who is abducted by a prince and ends up running a brothel in Africa. Midway through production of the planned four-hour epic, Swanson and Kennedy pulled the plug because Stroheim had driven the film way over budget; moreover, Swanson found Stroheim's attention to perverse details to be distasteful and thought the footage he was shooting was much too slow in preparation and excessive as well as unnecessary in the amount of film shot.[6] The decision to shelve the film cost Kennedy a great deal of money, and Stroheim's subsequent reputation as a director was ruined. Swanson's career rebounded nicely with Academy Award nominations in succession for *Sadie Thompson* (1928) and *The Trespasser* (1929). In fact, she continued to headline films until 1934 – several years into the sound era – and made one more film in 1941 before retiring from Hollywood. Swanson tried to salvage *Queen Kelly* by shooting new scenes but fought with Stroheim over ownership of his footage. A version of *Queen Kelly* was released abroad in 1932, but aside from the clip in *Sunset Boulevard*, it was not officially released in the US in anything resembling feature length until 1967; different cuts of *Queen Kelly* in abbreviated form now exist.

Following the debacle of *Queen Kelly* Stroheim continued to act, with a standout performance as a German officer in Jean Renoir's *Grand Illusion* (1937), although he also appeared in a number of uninspired films as well. Wilder himself had previously cast Stroheim as Field Marshall Erwin Rommel in *Five Graves to Cairo*. Stroheim bristled at what he considered the secondary role of Max and repeatedly made suggestions about his dialogue and bits of business for Max to do, most of which Wilder ignored. But it was Stroheim's idea that the butler wrote the numerous fan letters that Norma gets regularly; and he also suggested to Wilder that they use a clip from *Queen Kelly* for the silent film she and Joe watch.

In March, a month before shooting was to begin with the cast, Clift turned down the part, leaving the project in momentary disarray. He claimed that he could not convincingly make love to an older woman, as the script required, but there has always been speculation that at the time he was actually in a relationship with an older woman, torch singer Libby Holman, who had ordered him not to take the role. Names such as John Garfield and Burt Lancaster were tossed around but ultimately the part went to William Holden. Born William Beedle Jr, Holden's breakout role was as the violinist-turned-boxer in *Golden Boy* (1939) for Columbia, which shared his contract with Paramount. Military service in World War II had interrupted Holden's career and when he returned he was put in comedies and Westerns that traded on his good looks and athleticism. *Sunset Boulevard* would be a turning point in his career and his first of four films with Wilder, who became a close friend.

Since Holden was then thirty-one but playing a younger character of twenty-five, Swanson was told she would need to be aged with make-up. She declined, arguing that women of fifty who took good care of their looks did not look old, so why not make Holden youthful with make-up? They did a test and agreed with her. 'They changed Bill Holden's hair and adjusted his make-up and left me a spruced up fifty, which was exactly my age,' Swanson recalled in her memoir (1980: 481).

From late March until mid-April filming began with location shots: the county morgue and its exterior, the Sunset Strip, the outside of the Alto Nido apartment building, and other Hollywood and Beverly Hills locales (Sikov 1998: 293). Filming with the actors began on 18 April 1949, albeit without a complete script; but that was not unusual for a Wilder and Brackett production. While they were still working out script problems and uncertain about where to take some story points, the unfinished state of the screenplay allowed them to keep the nervous censors at the Production Code Administration (PCA) in the dark about the highly problematic narrative of the older woman maintaining a younger man as her lover, a turn of the plot that was absent in the pages initially submitted in March and April. The final pages that gave the PCA assurance of an unhappy ending for Joe and Norma were not sent until 18 July, at which point the script got the censors' approval. The PCA otherwise vetted just a few lines of dialogue (Joe could not tell Sheldrake he was 'up the creek' due to his desperate straits, nor was he allowed to say that the wind 'goosed' the organ in Norma's house) (Production Code Administration 1949).

Negotiations with Cecil B. DeMille for his important scene took place while the film continued shooting. Initially hoping that he would do his scene gratis, Brackett and Wilder finally agreed to pay him $10,000. 'He's well worth it,' Brackett wrote. But they would not meet the $20,000 asking price of Hedy Lamarr, the star of DeMille's *Samson and Delilah*, especially since she had initially agreed to a smaller fee of $1,500 (Slide 2015: 370). Her presence in the scene would supply the occasion for Norma taking Lamarr's chair on the set, but she could just as easily sit in DeMille's, as happens in the film.

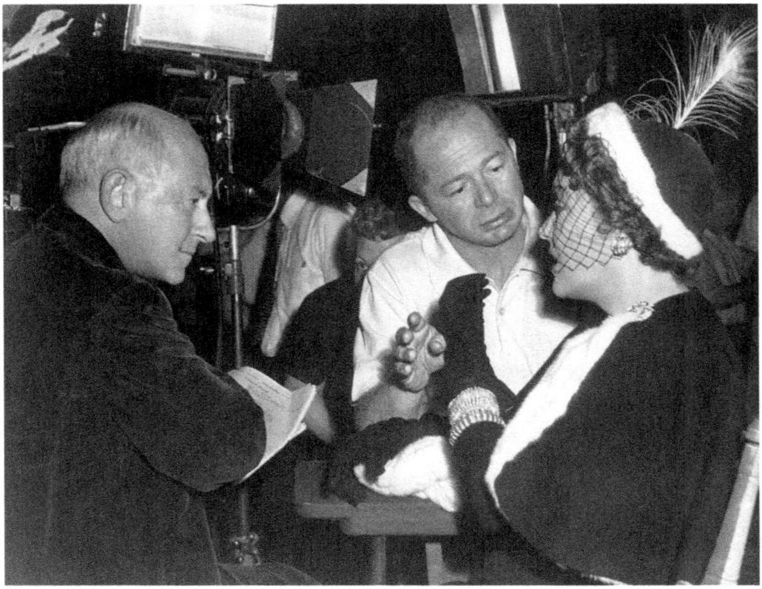

Cecil B. DeMille, Billy Wilder and Gloria Swanson

Additionally, Brackett and Wilder wanted both of the leading gossip columnists, Louella Parsons as well as Hedda Hopper. But an advance item in the *Hollywood Reporter*, probably planted by the studio, caused Parsons to believe Brackett was tricking her into appearing alongside her rival, and she refused to do the scene.

Throughout the shoot Brackett complained about the rushes in his diary. He thought John Seitz's lighting of scenes was too dark. He found that Fred Clark's nasty performance of Sheldrake 'makes our attitude about Hollywood snide and unworthy of the treatment Hollywood has given us' (Slide 2015: 374). He did not like Swanson's delivery of her speech about the movies. 'Billy assures me it will be so arresting in the sinister atmosphere of the house that it won't matter. He may be right but I feel she could be coached to something more human' (371). Brackett wanted to make Norma less arrogant, but he and Wilder also worried that a change in tone might throw the picture off balance. When they replaced the 'emotional Norma/DeMille scene' with 'a scene of arrogance on her part', Brackett worried it was 'another ice-cold scene in a chilly picture' (370–1). Later, after filming began and they were watching the rushes, Marshman, too, 'said, quite simply, "It just occurred to me this can be a picture that nobody will like"' (373). Watching the first rough cut, Brackett concluded, 'It's an uneven picture, interminably slow in parts, excellent when Swanson is involved, dull otherwise and lacking in emotion. If we can speed up the beginning it may be viable' (375).

At one point during production Wilder and crew played an affectionate joke on Swanson. She suggested her Charles Chaplin impersonation, which had been filmed but cut from *Manhandled* (1924), for the scene when Norma entertains a bored Joe. Wilder had fifty derbies brought in from wardrobe so she could choose one. On the day of filming, the crew and Wilder wore the remaining ones. Two days later, they shot the chimp's funeral scene. Swanson was told to remove the shawl covering the stuffed animal – and it too was wearing a derby (Swanson 1980: 483–4)! Wilder also played a trick on Holden. After getting what he wanted of the scene when Joe and

Norma's Chaplin

Betty kiss, Wilder asked Holden and Nancy Olson to do it again for protection. Knowing that Holden's wife was on set that day, Wilder did not yell 'cut', forcing the actors to hold their kiss – until Mrs Holden shouted 'cut'. She was not amused (Thomas 1983: 62).

But the script was not yet finished. The writers were still working out Norma's final moments. Originally, Max was to wake her from her trance by using the newsreel cameras as the strategy to get her to talk; but on the set Wilder agreed with Brackett's suggestion that the word 'cameras' should awaken her interest in her surroundings. In the evening, Wilder decided that her last speech would be 'a kind of happy madness, touching the sort of emotion we once had in the DeMille scene' (Slide 2015: 377). Brackett agreed, and they wrote it for filming the next day. Afterwards they had the cast party.

Then it turned out that filming was not yet finished. Brackett wanted Wilder to reshoot the close-up of Norma's 'I *am* big' speech and Joe's corresponding reaction shot, which was done in early July. Two days before, they had reshot the scene where Joe kisses Norma after her suicide attempt (Sikov 1998: 299). Holden now recorded his voiceover. 'Bill has a flat and uninteresting voice,' Brackett noted, 'but I think the commentary is pretty good' (Slide 2015: 380). The film was edited for sneak previews in September, first in Evanston, then almost immediately afterwards in Joliet and Poughkeepsie.

These previews were problematic. They revealed that the opening scene did not work as planned, for it failed to establish a proper tone for the film. In this original opening Joe's corpse is wheeled into the morgue where various corpses tell how they each died, leading into Joe's account of his death and the start of the long flashback to six months earlier, but this scene caused audience laughter as soon as a name tag was placed on Holden's big toe. In a story he repeated many times in other interviews, too, Wilder recalled to Cameron Crowe that 'people got up and left. I left too. I went down some steps, leading to the toilets, and I looked up and

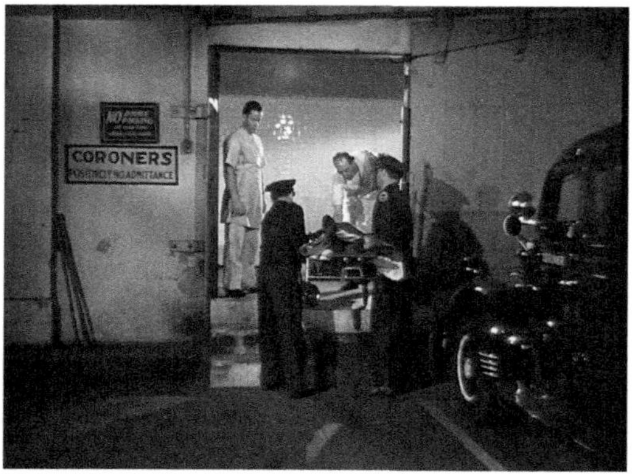

The arrival of Joe's corpse at the morgue in the deleted prologue

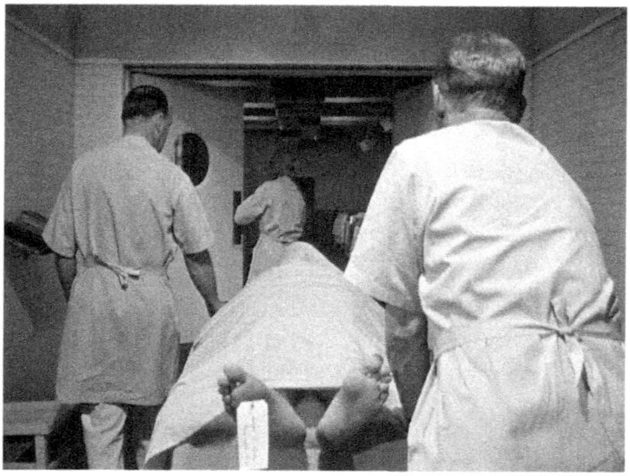

there was a lady with a spring hat on, in her sixties, and she turned to me, and she said, "Have you ever seen such shit in your life?" And I said, "Frankly no".' Crowe records Wilder's own laughter after his recounting of this story (1999: 255).

As well as jettisoning the morgue frame and crafting a new opening, more reshoots of key scenes were in order. Along with the writers' reworking of the voiceover commentary, new filming took place in mid-October. They shot footage of cop cars on Sunset Boulevard at dawn for the new opening, redid the tricky shot of Joe floating face down in the pool, and filmed again the scene where Norma hires Joe. Additionally, Brackett wrangled with Wilder 'to try and get some warmth into the DeMille scene'. DeMille had critiqued the latest cut to Brackett, who agreed 'with his urgent feeling that Norma should be humanized and made normal at the beginning' (Slide 2015: 384). Wilder initially bristled at DeMille's criticism but eventually reworked the scene where the director says goodbye to Norma outside the soundstage. Before agreeing to return to the set, DeMille got a $6,000 Cadillac limo and a $3,000 bonus (Sikov 1998: 300).

A new cut of *Sunset Boulevard* was previewed in Oakland in late October, followed by a second one in Redwood City; both confirmed the film had been improved. But the final scene was still not right, since, according to Brackett, it needed 'some semblance of realism with the definite implication that she's to be carted off to the county psychiatric ward as soon as her big scene is over' (Slide 2015: 389). At first resisting, Wilder agreed to reshoot. On 5 January 1950, production reopened. Wilder first shot nine different versions of the conversation between the two detectives; then he had Swanson perform her descent down the staircase ten times, each time adopting a different expression and posture, and different arm gestures. As in the days of silent movie-making, Wilder had musical accompaniment for Swanson's acting: 'The Dance of the Seven Veils' from the Strauss opera *Salome*. Six takes were in medium long shot; four were taken with the camera placed further back (Sikov 1998: 300–1). On film the

The End
A Paramount Picture

final shot famously ends with Swanson walking towards the camera until her close-up gets fuzzy, dissolving to the end credits. Cameron Crowe asked Wilder if he had used an optical effect as Swanson got closer to the camera but the director said no. 'The focus gets thrown out by the focus carrier,' Wilder explained. 'I left the camera running. I didn't know where to cut' (1999: 151).

Wilder was not a showy director. In *Sunset Boulevard* he for the most part avoided the unusual camera angles typical of other film noirs of the postwar period and instead followed conventions of continuity editing, relying on long takes of medium or medium wide shots intercut with shot/reverse shot close-ups to showcase the snappy dialogue. Tighter close-ups were reserved for key moments, such as the two-shot when the salesman whispers that Joe should take the vicuña coat since the lady is paying, or when Norma hears the word 'cameras'. Establishing shots were likewise used sparingly, as in the overhead long shot of the vast soundstage teeming with people working for DeMille before Norma arrives, or the overhead shot of Joe and Norma dancing the tango at her New Year's Eve party; or such shots that affirm Joe's viewpoint by disclosing what he sees in the distance, as in his first glimpse of Norma's mansion and then of her calling out to him from the second-floor balcony. Wilder always maintained that the best directing was invisible, serving the script, which was paramount for him.

In order to learn directing, Wilder had agreed to co-write *Ball of Fire* for Sam Goldwyn with the condition that he be allowed on the set to watch Howard Hawks direct. According to Sikov, Wilder emulates the Hawksian style. 'At no point does Wilder ever yank his audience's attention away from his characters toward self-aggrandising, showoff visual effects. Such ostentatious finger pointing simply isn't Wilder's style. From watching Howard Hawks, Wilder learned to shoot in ways both formally strict and relaxedly invisible' (1998: 177). Wilder himself idolised Ernst Lubitsch, and it was that director, not Hawks, that Wilder talked about with admiration. He famously kept a placard with the query 'What would Lubitsch do?'

on his office wall, and to Crowe he declared that Hawks did *not* influence him (1999: 192).[7] However, as Sikov points out, the proof is in the image: 'Lubitsch imprinted himself onto every frame; Hawks effaced himself.' But Hawks 'knew not only what every shot would be like but also how each of these pieces would fit together in a seamless flow of images' (1998: 162). Wilder filmed the same way, as he more or less admitted. 'Hawks didn't mind my hanging around, like a fly on the wall,' Wilder told Charlotte Chandler. 'I didn't set out to be like him, but something might have rubbed off' (2002: 100).

On *Sunset Boulevard* Wilder worked with his favourite cutter, Doane Harrison, who functioned on this film, as on Wilder's earlier and some later ones, as editorial supervisor before being elevated to associate producer, beginning with the director's *The Seven Year Itch* (1955). Years later Wilder would recall that he 'learned a great deal' from Harrison because when he started directing, 'my technical knowledge was very meagre'. Harrison taught Wilder how

Charles Brackett, Billy Wilder and Doane Harrison, c. mid-1940s

to pre-plan shots to form an overall scheme, without many protection shots, and to shoot the way he thinks a scene should look (Staggs 2002: 148), much as Wilder had watched Hawks edit in his mind as he set up shots for *Ball of Fire*.

Wilder likewise had for *Sunset Boulevard* the same director of cinematography, John F. Seitz, who had worked with him previously on *Double Indemnity*, considered one of the first film noirs, as well as on *Five Graves to Cairo* and *The Lost Weekend*. Whereas Harrison was on set with Wilder as consultant, Seitz would light a scene and turn his back to the action or clear out entirely, apparently phobic about watching the actors perform (Staggs 2002: 124). Seitz used low-key lighting to create the shadowy atmosphere of Norma's mansion, where nothing is quite what it seems when Joe first arrives. Watching the rushes, producer Brackett complained several times in his diary that the footage was dark and 'badly lighted' because Seitz was 'not a topnotch cameraman' (Slide 2015: 371–2). But Wilder and Seitz appeared to know what they wanted. Adding to the Gothic atmosphere of Norma's mansion, Seitz blew magnesium dust into the air of the soundstage that 'photographed like motes in sunbeams', as Wilder is said to have remembered (Staggs 2002: 121).

In an article on Seitz's lighting of *Sunset Boulevard* published at the time of its release, the *American Cinematographer* described how the film 'depends upon photographic mood for much of its dramatic effect. Thus, the more intense sequences are played in a low-key faithfully motivated by time of day as well as locale.' Although the writer does not specify which sequence he has in mind, he notes how the key light illuminating the actors appears to come from a lamp in the composition, with 'a minimum of fill-light being used to soften the shadows. This might be described as *source* lighting carried to the ultimate degree' (Lightman 1950: 318). Aside from its dark narrative, which shall be discussed in the next chapter, *Sunset Boulevard*'s status as a film noir is primarily due to the 'low-key', shadowy atmosphere of Norma's house, created by the lighting, the set design and a handful of other shots planned for their macabre or ominous effect.

The daylight setting of the opening scenes contrasts with the more dimly lit interior of Norma's mansion, where shadows play along the walls, and source lighting comes from candles in wall sconces and candelabras or lamps with ornate fringed shades, creating the oppressive, claustrophobic effect of the house as a dungeon where the former star is held captive by her memories, guarded by her faithful, stone-faced, Germanic butler. In the early scene of Joe approaching the derelict-looking mansion he is bathed in sunlight, his face and body clearly delineated, while in the next shot bamboo venetian blinds obscure Norma as she looks down at him from the second floor. In an atypical shot for Wilder, the camera moves towards her quickly, its rapid motion creating an uneasy, unsettling feeling. Max greets Joe and instructs him to enter, and the shot is again brightly lit, but as Joe goes upstairs, the camera lingers on Max in close-up watching Joe ascend, followed by a medium wide shot of the writer as he climbs the dimly lit stairs and reaches the darkened landing. Not knowing where to go, Joe turns in one direction but Norma orders from off screen, 'this way.' She stands just outside her bedroom, the only illumination in the hallway coming from a flickering candle on a wall sconce, and she draws Joe into the darkness as she instructs, 'in here,' leading him into her baroquely furnished bedchamber.

Holden has more close-ups in this next scene, as he registers surprise at what Norma says and when he sees the chimp in its coffin; ostensibly because he is standing in the shadows, fill lighting moulds the contours of Holden's face, giving his handsome visage an impression of dimensionality and visual complexity, including the reflection on his greased hair of a very thin slice of light from a wall sconce behind him. By comparison, Swanson's first close-up in this scene lacks the diffused look of conventional glamour lighting, presumably because she stands in the glare of the room's artificial light. When she removes her dark glasses, the harsh light flattens Swanson's face, giving it the appearance of a mask; her skin is smooth and unlined except for under her eyes and the crease on each cheek. A medium wide shot then shows both actors facing each other;

Holden backs away, only to turn round again when he recognises her, declaring, 'You're Norma Desmond. You used to be big.' When Norma declares that she *is* big and 'it's the pictures that got small,' and then continues angrily to belittle the industry, the tighter close-ups of her face now more closely reflect the diffused glamour lighting befitting a female star, moulding her face with a fill lamp (and possibly evidence of the final set of retakes that Brackett noted in his diary). Harsher lighting returns in subsequent medium wide shots as Norma chases Joe out of the room and downstairs, only to call him back and lead him into her parlour once she learns he is a writer.

To give another example of how the lighting creates a noir mood while also directing us where and how to look: in the later scene when they watch the *Queen Kelly* excerpt, in a medium shot Joe and Norma sit in the shadows with the light from the projector beam aimed above their heads, as his voiceover describes her as an enrapt fan of her own movies. This composition sets up the moment when, complaining that producers no longer know what faces are, Norma stands and proclaims her determination to return to the screen; although still in

darkness, the beam of light coming from the projector illuminates the back of her head so that the outline of her hair shimmers in the dusty air as cigarette smoke wafts up towards her face. When she stops speaking, she defiantly turns her head, the beam of light now highlighting her profile, which dissolves to a high-angled long shot omnisciently looking down on her and the waxworks playing bridge.

The scene in *Sunset Boulevard* that perhaps most closely resembles conventional film noir occurs towards the end, when Max meets Joe in the garage after the latter returns from a writing session with Betty at Paramount. Max warns Joe that Norma is awake and watching out for him, and then reveals his own history as a promising director, discoverer of Norma when she was in her teens, and her first husband. Filmed in close-up, the faces of Holden and Stroheim are sliced by shadows, the gloomy space of the garage behind them barely discernible.

The shots that most call attention to Wilder's virtuosity occur in the opening. As Joe's flashback begins we see a busy street and the camera moves to the exterior of the Alto Nido apartments;

it travels from the street towards an open window on the second floor, curtains gently blowing in the breeze; with a cut, the camera looks voyeuristically through the open window, where in a medium shot Joe is in his bathrobe, typing. It is worth noting that Wilder had used a similar voyeuristic opening in *The Lost Weekend* to show the bottle of liquor hanging by a rope outside the window before moving the camera through the opening to record Philip Terry's dialogue with his alcoholic brother, played by Ray Milland.[8]

More striking is how Wilder shows Joe's corpse face down in the pool from 'a fish's perspective', as uniformed cops, plainclothes detectives and photographers inspect and photograph the body and drag it out of the pool. This was tricky to achieve and was finally resolved by John Meehan, one of the two credited art directors. At the bottom of a tank was an 8-by-6-foot mirror. The actors playing the police and photographers were filmed against a muslin canopy, which in black-and-white cinematography created the impression of a dawn sky. The water itself had to be well filtered and ice cold for clarity in the filming (which made it very uncomfortable

for Holden). Seitz then lit the scene, pointing the camera down at the mirror below and filmed Holden's reflection (Sikov 1998: 299; Staggs 2002: 85).

Before *Sunset Boulevard* became a stage musical, music was already a crucial element, underscoring the script and Wilder's direction. At some point during the early summer, Franz Waxman, who had known Wilder from their time together in Berlin, began to work on his haunting musical score, what Staggs calls 'a sonata in noir', with snatches of jazz, the tango, the blues and 'Stravinskyian throbs and thrusts' (2002: 141–2). Notice how the score correlates to characterisation, with a contemporary jazzy bebop theme for Joe and a Latin tango for Norma evocative of the Jazz Age and Valentino. At times the arrangement features a solo instrument for emotional emphasis, such as a saxophone, oboe, flute, percussion or strings.

Waxman textured his score with wit, too. The tango theme melodically deteriorates to underscore Norma's growing insanity and tense emotional state; for example, a 'gypsy violin' frantically plays over the tango during the montage of her rigorous cosmetic preparation for her 'return' to the screen. In the scene when Norma rises while watching *Queen Kelly* to declare that she *will* return to the screen, Waxman momentarily borrows from his own score for *The Bride of Frankenstein* (1935). If *Sunset Boulevard* seems like a monster movie at times, as Ed Sikov suggests at this point in his commentary on the 2002 DVD and 2012 Blu-ray, that sense is not only due to the lighting, as Sikov reasons, but is cued by Waxman's appropriation of a bit of his own horror music for this moment. Likewise, the love theme for Joe and Betty, played as they stroll the backlot, includes a slowed-down, parodic version of the studio's 'Paramount on Parade', a song from its 1930 all-star review of that same title, which was subsequently used as a march in its newsreels and promotional reels. Before then, as underscoring for the scene when Norma entertains a bored Joe, whom she senses is bothered by something, this theme anticipates his close-up and voiceover confession moments later that he has been thinking about Betty and the script she wants to write.

With the film finally in the can, Paramount began to arrange private 'invitation only' screenings in Los Angeles to create buzz. Before the film opened in August, twenty-one of these had taken place. The one people remember and that is included in almost every account of *Sunset Boulevard*, Wilder's biography and Swanson's happened early on. It was a star-studded affair of three hundred people, prefaced by a dinner party for an exclusive group, including Swanson, at Louis B. Mayer's home. After the film ended, as Swanson recalled, 'the whole audience stood up and cheered'. Barbara Stanwyck kissed the hem of Swanson's skirt in admiration of her fearless performance. Mary Pickford was supposedly so moved and teary-eyed that she slipped out of a side door so that no one would see her. 'She's overcome,' someone told Swanson. 'We all are' (Swanson 1980: 484–5).

Not everyone was so overcome, however. Mayer, the head of MGM, was furious, shouting at Wilder that his film disgraced the industry that had made and fed him, and that he should be tarred and feathered and run out of town. Wilder's terse response was either 'Fuck you' or 'Go shit in your hat,' depending on the remembered account (Sikov 1998: 303). What angered him most was that Mayer, a Middle European Jew like himself, had excluded Brackett from his tirade, ignoring the Protestant Republican and singling out for his rage the Jewish liberal émigré.

With that kind of heightened response by Hollywood insiders, clearly *Sunset Boulevard* was now ready for its close-up.

3 'A Hollywood Story'

Along with its ghostly voiceover, *Sunset Boulevard* is 'a most unusual motion picture' because of its backstudio narrative.[9] Many movies about Hollywood and the film industry appeared in the 1920s and 30s, but their protagonists – as the main characters in two of the most famous backstudio pictures, Mary Evans (Constance Bennett) in *What Price Hollywood?* (1932) and Esther Blodgett (Janet Gaynor) in *A Star Is Born* (1937), illustrate – were for the most part young women whose stories trace the slow progress and the steep price of becoming film stars.[10] Significantly, too, and again like Mary and Esther, most of the young female characters in early backstudios are initially drawn to Hollywood because of their fandom. Those two landmark backstudios, moreover, pair their young female protagonists, their stardom on the rise, with more experienced Hollywood men – Max Carey (Lowell Sherman) in *What Price Hollywood?* and Norman Maine (Fredric March) in *A Star Is Born* – whose careers implode due to their drinking and outlandish public behaviour, and both male characters end up committing suicide. In *Hollywood Boulevard* (1936), another former movie star, John Blakeford (John Halliday), has been out of work and broke since the industry made its full conversion to sound in 1929, but he revives his moribund career with the serial publication of his memoir in the tabloid press – with salacious bits added by the publisher. In *It Happened in Hollywood* (1937), cowboy star Tim Bart (Richard Dix) also loses his job when his studio converts to talkies, but off-screen heroics revive his career and, according to this movie, save the Western genre to boot.

Despite the number of prior backstudios about stardom made to promote Hollywood as a dream factory, none featured a narrative with a fifty-year-old woman like Norma Desmond as the main character. However, older women whose careers had diminished because of age appeared as secondary characters in two backstudios from the 1930s. In *Show Girl in Hollywood* (1930), Donny Harris (Blanche Sweet) is, like Norma, a former star now forgotten by the industry. Washed up in pictures at thirty-two, she feels 'older than the hills up there', she tells the protagonist, the youthful starlet Dixie Dugan (Alice White) – because 'you can't lie before the camera'. *Music Is Magic* (1935), a backstudio starring top-billed Alice Faye as a stage performer trying to break into pictures, features another character who anticipates Norma Desmond. 'I'd like her a lot better if she stopped trying to be sixteen years old,' a fan says of movie star Diane De Valle (Bebe Daniels). Yet despite the number of fans who have turned up their noses at her because they see through her pose, Diane continues playing young; she even forces her grown daughter, Shirley, to pass as her sister and, simply out of vanity (since she does not care for the man very deeply), keeps on a short leash a wealthy young suitor whom the daughter secretly loves. But when an accident on set endangers Shirley's life, Diane finally acknowledges her daughter's identity and hence her real age in front of the entire studio community.

Sunset Boulevard may not have been the first backstudio to reflect Hollywood's ageism but it was the first to wrap a narrative entirely around a mature actress left behind by the film industry, a character who does not capitulate to patriarchal Hollywood (as Donny and Dixie both do in *Show Girl in Hollywood*) or accept maternal roles supporting a younger star (as Diane does at the end of *Music Is Magic*). Hollywood has forgotten Norma because of her age but also because the arrival of talkies initiated a dramatic shift in acting styles. As Norma herself exclaims after declaring that she *is* big and 'it's the pictures that got small,' her voice clipping the words as she utters them: 'There was a time when this business had the eyes of the whole wide world. But that wasn't good enough. Oh no! They wanted the ears of the world, too. So they opened their big mouths, and out came talk, talk, talk.' This difference sets up a trope through performance that contrasts Norma and the younger Joe Gillis, who writes scripts composed of dialogue and whose voiceover is nothing but 'talk, talk, talk'.

Norma's mansion, Joe says in voiceover, is 'like that old woman in *Great Expectations*, that Miss Havisham in her rotting wedding dress and torn veil, taking it out on the world because she's been given the go-by'. His allusion to Charles Dickens's *Great Expectations* implies that the decaying exterior will be mirrored by the person inside, so it determines how we seem meant to see Norma before she appears. The big house looks run-down, the garage doors imperfectly hung, the pool empty except for rats. When Joe hides his car in Norma's spacious garage, he sees an expensive foreign automobile sitting there with a 1932 licence plate, its wheels resting on bricks, and he assumes that must be the year the owners moved out of the place, leaving it empty. Inside the house, the rooms are dark, dusty and overdecorated, and an organ wheezes whenever the wind gets into its pipes. Time has stood still for that Dickens's character, just as it has for Norma Desmond. Still, Joe's voiceover establishes a perspective that favours the present over the past, taking as a given that the talkies and present-day Hollywood, which gave the 'go-by' to Norma some twenty years before, are superior to silent cinema and the kind of larger-than-life stardom it created, which she personifies.

This viewpoint is the privilege of living in the present moment, as Joe does (albeit ironically, since he *is* dead, after all). It ignores how Hollywood's past and its present are, simply, different; the coming of sound caused an epochal change in the film industry that made silent films and the talkies seem like different species of entertainment. (In fact, the screen ratio changed slightly with the addition of optical soundtracks, and while the speed of silents varied, leading to the jerkiness of many when first shown on early television, sound films were regulated at the standard twenty-four frames per second.) The difference is reinforced through the acting styles of Billy Wilder's two stars and his direction of them.

By 1950, a time just before Method acting called attention to the craft and training of a film performer, the acting style favoured by Hollywood once the industry learned how to use sound technology with finesse resembled William Holden's in both his performance of Joe and his voiceover: naturalistic because somewhat restrained, especially when it came to delivering dialogue, giving the impression that a performer was not acting but simply 'being' the part. Dialogue simulated ordinary speech to accentuate the actor's naturalism. Films were crafted around a star's screen persona, drawing elements from it for a character, which further reinforced an illusion of transparency on the performer's part. *Sunset Boulevard* was not a star vehicle but Holden had been a product of the studio system since his breakout role in *Golden Boy*. Notice how he subtly uses his face and voice to express astonishment, bemusement, superiority, irritation or humiliation in his interactions with Gloria Swanson.

Conversely, without spoken dialogue, the performance style of early cinema required broad, sweeping, heightened, often seemingly (to more modern eyes) excessive displays of face and body to convey the truth of a character through mime. Evoking the miming style of acting and with it the forgotten aura of silent cinema, Swanson inflects Norma's speeches – as deliberately calibrated as Joe's although their cadences differ – to highlight the flourishes of her movement, as when she rises from a chair, moves across the room or stands in defiance to declare that she *will* be up on the screen again. Similarly, she curls her mouth and opens her eyes wide or lowers them to express emotion, and she uses her animated hands like claws for visual emphasis, whether to grasp the wire cigarette holder near her face, to punctuate her speech or to draw Holden into an embrace. In her demeanour, and hand and facial gestures, Norma often speaks and acts as if she lives inside a silent film.

Notice Swanson's acting, for instance, when she fears she is losing Joe for good. Before entering his bedroom where he is packing to return to Ohio, she first stops in front of a mirror to remove the cosmetic tapes on her cheeks and forehead and adjust her face, as if

preparing to go on stage; once inside the room, she acts expansively with her face and body even while speaking dialogue. By comparison, if Norma's emotions are not worked up because she feels in control, as when she hires Joe to edit her script, he interrupts her at bridge when his car is getting towed or she towels him down after he goes swimming, Swanson's delivery is more measured and evenly pitched, her movement regal and self-possessed.

Through their differently styled performances, Swanson and Holden enact two different Hollywoods as personified by their characters: his low-key, naturalistic performance measures by comparison the oversized and baroque style that Swanson uses to depict Norma's estrangement from the present.[11] This may be another sense in which the pictures have 'got small' while she remains big, larger than life. With its cloistered atmosphere and opulent if outmoded decor, the mansion functions as the perfect setting for Norma's often histrionic performance of a silent screen heroine; she may have once known how to play to the camera, but now she has to settle for playing to her room.

Norma first appears in *Sunset Boulevard* calling out to Joe in a voice-off, 'Why are you so late? Why have you kept me waiting so long?' Norma thinks he is the tardy undertaker come to bury her dead pet chimpanzee but, given her belief that as a star she is eternally youthful and awaits the industry's invitation for her to 'return', she may as well be asking the same two questions of modern-day Hollywood. Following Joe's point of view, the camera looks towards the mansion and shows her peering at him from behind bamboo blinds; dark glasses conceal her eyes and a raised hand obscures her face. When Joe enters the mansion and meets her there – her figure dressed in black daytime pyjamas, a leopard-print turban on her head with a matching scarf, several glittering bracelets adorning one wrist, her eyes still hidden by those dark glasses – Norma remains in shadows, half her face covered by the dimness.

As I began to discuss in the second chapter, the visual contrast between Norma's darkened abode, lit by artificial lighting, and the bright daylight outside, made striking by the reverse shot back to Joe after she calls out to him from the second-floor window, establishes how the *mise en scène* of Norma's gloomy yet grand house will characterise her throughout *Sunset Boulevard*. She uses her seclusion as a cloak to protect her from the contemporary world outside; the thick drapes, the heavy furniture, the ornate lampshades and dimly lit wall sconces, the high ceilings, the oriental rugs and marble floors, the numerous photographs and portraits of her youthful visage everywhere you look, all work to reinforce the visual impression that, much as Joe's allusion to Miss Havisham proposes, the mansion cushions Norma from the reality that she has been forgotten by the industry.

Joe's voiceover underscores what that *mise en scène* suggests about Norma being an anachronism in 1950. His running commentary, which at points is self-effacing but as often self-congratulatory, implies that he controls the narrative; his voiceover seeks to determine how we are to think about and respond to Norma.

The eloquence of his witty commentary – a mosaic of wisecracks, literary allusions, colourful street lingo, insightful descriptions – encourages us to see Norma from the distance marked by his perspective, but it is nonetheless a partial viewpoint. If, as Karen McNally rightly observes, Joe is an unreliable narrator unable to appreciate Norma's sympathetic figure until the film's climax, I think Wilder's cynicism, which laces the screenplay, still views both Joe's unreliable narration and Norma's melodramatically inflected stardom with irony, which densifies and complicates Wilder's 'reverence for a long-lost movie stardom' (2021: 58).

After he moves into the mansion, Joe brings Norma into closer contact with the outside world. She has the swimming pool cleaned and filled for him to use, and has her Isotta-Fraschini restored; functioning now as her chauffeur as well as her butler, Max drives the couple around Beverly Hills and Hollywood. These trips highlight Joe's degradation. Norma does not like his clothes so she has Max take them to an expensive men's shop in Beverly Hills where she buys Joe new suits, a tuxedo and a topcoat. Joe prefers a camel-hair coat but the salesman condescendingly whispers, 'As long as the lady is paying for it, why not take the vicuña?' Joe curtly replies, 'The camel hair will do.' The more expensive and luxurious vicuña coat is the outward sign, as the salesman knows, that Joe is Norma's kept man. We soon learn that Joe has taken the vicuña when Artie Green comments on the feel of the coat's sumptuous material at the New Year's Eve party.

Then, after Norma's suicide attempt, she and Joe are on the way to play bridge with the waxworks when they stop at Schwab's drugstore for him to buy her cigarettes. There he runs into Betty and Artie, who are eating supper at the soda fountain counter. Betty again asks Joe to collaborate with her on the script based on his 'Dark Windows' flashback when Max enters the drugstore to summon Joe, who obediently departs. Both times Joe encounters Artie – at the New Year's Eve party and in Schwab's – his friend makes jokes about the mysterious life Joe must be living, given his tailored tuxedo and

vicuña coat (at the party) and the foreign-sounding gentleman who orders him to leave (in the drugstore).

The most important trip Norma and Joe take away from the mansion is to Paramount studios. Norma's encounter with Cecil B. DeMille on the soundstage happens outside Joe's ken – and his voiceover – because he does not accompany her but waits outside by the car with Max until he sees Betty strolling to her cubicle. The scenes at Paramount provide a deeper perspective on Norma, on the industry, on Hollywood's history. Soundstages were a requirement when studios converted from silent pictures to talkies because the enclosed space enabled the integrity of dialogue to be recorded directly and without accidental interference during filming. Here on stage 18 we see film-making occurring in all its size and complexity, with extras in biblical costumes, assorted technicians and various assistants moving about the expansive space. DeMille is directing *Samson and Delilah*, first rehearsing, then filming a scene with Henry Wilcoxon, who has a supporting role in the director's actual movie.

Amidst all this hustle and bustle we see Hollywood's patriarchy at work, too. DeMille is older than Norma, as he tells his assistant ('I could be her father,' he grumbles), nearly seventy, yet he is still running the show. Unlike Norma, Wilcoxon, who began as a leading man in the 1930s – he played Antony in the director's *Cleopatra* (1934) – sustained a lengthy career, transitioning to smaller supporting parts as he aged, and he would go on to serve as associate producer on DeMille's last three films. Hog-Eye, who operates the overhead light, remembers Norma from working with her in the past, as do many of the extras on the set.[12] Furthermore, one has to note the off-screen irony that the huge success of *Samson and Delilah* prompted the cycle of biblical epics that dominated the 1950s. Norma's script, while bloated and overwrought, anticipates this cycle. (And while Norma is too old to play the young temptress of her imagination, Columbia did make a version of *Salome* in 1953 starring Rita Hayworth.)

At the end of this scene, DeMille tells Norma to watch him film. 'You know, pictures have changed quite a bit.' This scene at Paramount visually places her in an antagonistic relation to those changes (remember her early diatribe against 'talk, talk, talk'); a boom mic dangles over her head, knocking the white ostrich feather in her hat, until she angrily pushes the microphone away with her gloved hand. All the same, the visit causes Norma to tear up because it makes her realise what she has missed – not only the work but the adulation. From an overhead scaffold the electrician Hog-Eye sees Norma and illuminates her figure in a spotlight; people on set, mostly old-timers, cluster around her as one voice mutters, 'I thought she was dead,' while another murmurs, 'welcome home, Miss Desmond.' Those two voices reiterate the conflict that arose when Norma arrived at the front gate. The young guard fails to recognise her ('Norma who?' he asks), but the older guard Jonesy remembers her and informs the younger man, 'Miss Desmond doesn't need a pass.' As Max drives through, Norma tells Jonesy to remind his colleague that 'without me there wouldn't be a Paramount studio'.

The moment is complexly layered. The guarded entrance at the famous Bronson Gate of Paramount keeps outsiders away while letting insiders onto the lot. Norma's difficulty in getting by the young guard epitomises her banishment from Hollywood because 'pictures have changed quite a bit'. Those changes have to do with the infrastructure of film-making as well as the technological innovations occasioned by sound. In 1948 the federal government's successful anti-trust case against Paramount by name and the other majors implicitly (as 'et al.') broke up the studio system by forcing divestiture of their exhibition chains, the source of their profits; weekly attendance at movie theatres, at all-time highs during the war years and immediately afterwards, started its ominous decline; and early television was already perceived as a rival, drawing away those moviegoers. Studios began thinking twice about renewing the long-term contracts, not only of major stars but of other above-the-line employees like writers; they would cease making 'B' pictures (the kind of movie Joe Gillis had been writing), since without theatre chains they did not have the financial incentive to fill houses with

double bills each week; with their annual production slates reduced, independent production companies and freelance actors, writers and directors started to become the standard. Moreover, studios began producing big, expensive Technicolorful epics sold for their spectacle (like DeMille's *Samson and Delilah*) in order to compete with television and its small pictures.

Once inside stage 18 Norma exclaims to DeMille that she doesn't care about the money, she just wants to work again. But despite her desperation to work, and her willingness either to forgo her salary or possibly to finance the production of 'Salome' herself, she immediately slips back into her prima donna mode, declaring matter-of-factly, 'And remember, darling, that I don't work before ten in the morning and never after 4:30 in the afternoon.' No longer can the industry tolerate the self-indulgent behaviour of old-time stars like Norma. On the other hand, Norma's stardom, like Swanson's in real life, was fundamental to the establishment of Paramount as the first major Hollywood studio. The guarded front gate thus also symbolises the insular world of film-making that once supported movie stars like Norma, creating their larger-than-life personae, protecting them by ensuring their privacy and underwriting their lavish, self-indulgent lifestyles with huge salaries.

Despite her turn from narcissistic self-absorption to madness and murder in the final reel, *Sunset Boulevard* makes Norma a figure of great pathos because we know her script, incoherent and cluttered with 'those wild hallucinations of hers', as Joe remarks, will never be filmed, just as it is obvious that she deceives herself into believing she has not been forgotten by those millions of fans supposedly eager for her to return to the screen. DeMille says her script is 'awful' but wants to let her down gently, adding that he won't 'give her the brush' as her fans have done. Much later, in the final moments Joe's voiceover speculates about 'those headlines [that] would kill her', ranging from 'Crime of Passion, Temporary Insanity', to 'Forgotten Star a Slayer', 'Ageing Actress', 'Yesterday's Glamour Queen'. Norma's madness intensifies her pathos, for it will prevent her from registering the devastating impact of such cruel phrases. Adding to her pathos at the end is her expression of joy about returning to the cameras when she thinks Max is DeMille directing her in 'Salome'. She fails to see that she is surrounded, not by a film crew, but by newsreel men, reporters and police, and that the camera is recording her humiliating arrest. At the same time, she addresses 'those wonderful people out there in the dark' – we, the viewing audience – who are encouraged to share in her fantasy, the fantasy that is the movies.

Max's substituting for DeMille in those final moments crystallises how he has helped to make Norma this figure of pathos. As her servant, he works hard to sustain the illusion that history has not given Norma 'the go-by'. Max keeps reminding her that she was the greatest of stars, just as, by forging the scores of fan letters she gets daily, he perpetuates her belief in the currency of her stardom. Paradoxically, though, his character amplifies the historical conditions that doomed silent-era stars like Norma to extinction.

The cryptic, unemotional and seemingly omnipresent Max Von Mayerling is not the cipher he first seems, obedient to Madame's every wish and whim. As *Sunset Boulevard* moves towards its powerful conclusion, Max informs Joe that he was Norma's first director when she was a teenager, and, with DeMille and D. W. Griffith, one of the three most promising talents of the early medium. What is more, Max reveals that he was Norma's first husband! Joe is visibly surprised at this new information (as a first-time viewer usually is, too). Max tells Joe that he willingly returned as her servant because life without Norma was intolerable. Through his subservient position, which seems humiliating to Joe, Max draws his lifeblood from memories of Norma's stardom; he takes pleasure and pride when recounting to Joe stories of the men who threw themselves at Norma because of her powerful sexuality as a screen icon, an erotic allure both she and Max assume still burns hot. Max's backstory reminds us of the centrality of female stardom to Hollywood, indicating how the system – professionally (as her former director) and personally (as her first husband) – exploited young women like

Norma while creating for them an illusion of their empowerment and immortality as movie stars, which encourages us to see her pathos and emotionally complicates the ending when Joe's attempt to leave starts her descent from self-deception to utter madness.

The play of Hollywood's artifice with real locations and people throughout *Sunset Boulevard* reflects how fantasy and reality clash in Norma's life, and the blurring of those boundaries may encourage one to sympathise with this fallen star, despite her mental fragility (Trowbridge 2002: 303). As in earlier backstudios, Billy Wilder uses the actual locations of his film's production – the soundstages and backlot at Paramount – as well as footage of actual Los Angeles streets as the setting for events happening in the diegesis, just as several Hollywood people play themselves alongside fictional characters.

An awareness of the visual stitching used to create the film's verisimilitude resonates from the opening title cards, shot on the real Sunset Boulevard, to the finale when the real Hedda Hopper phones the city desk of the *Los Angeles Times*, the real major LA

newspaper where her daily gossip column ran, and a real Paramount newsreel truck is parked outside Norma's mansion. Real-life people like Hopper, DeMille and Wilcoxon appear as themselves; former silent stars Buster Keaton, H. B. Warner and Anna Q. Nilsson play the waxworks. In the background at Artie's New Year party, songwriters Ray Evans and Jay Livingston perform on a piano a snippet of their Oscar-winning song, 'Button and Bows', written for Paramount's *The Paleface* (1948). Passing reference to dead and living Hollywood stars like Greta Garbo, Rudolph Valentino, Mabel Normand, Wallace Reid, Charles Chaplin, John Gilbert, Betty Hutton, Alan Ladd and Tyrone Power pepper the dialogue.

Adding to this self-reflexivity, when Joe and Norma watch one of her films the excerpt is from *Queen Kelly*, that notorious unfinished and unreleased silent film starring and produced by Swanson and directed by Stroheim. At Paramount, Max points out to Joe the row of offices that was once Norma's expansive dressing room suite; on the second floor was his own office when he directed, he recalls, its walls 'covered in black patent leather'. That second floor has since been converted into cubicles in the readers' department, where Betty Schaefer works vetting scripts for producers like Sheldrake. Much as the writers' 'talk, talk, talk' displaced the silent star's face – and the excerpted scene features mainly close-ups of a young Swanson – the studio system, which matured with the coming of sound, made obsolete the kind of self-indulgent director Max personified in his heyday, if the clip of the unreleased *Queen Kelly* directed by his portrayer is any indication.

The scenes at Paramount are the most obviously self-reflexive. They were shot at the studio shortly after DeMille completed *Samson and Delilah*. The sets had not yet been struck, so the interior of soundstage 18 is, in effect, a set of a set in which the director performed 'directing' for director Billy Wilder. Furthermore, with the exception of the avuncular DeMille, everyone with a speaking part at Paramount, from the guards to Hog-Eye to DeMille's assistants and Gordon Cole, were actors.

Similarly, when Joe and Betty begin writing together at Paramount, the night-time scenes were shot in the evening at the studio. If the writing stalls, the couple stroll 'the drowsy lot', Joe tells us, 'just wandering down alleys between the soundstages or through the sets they were getting ready for the next day's shooting'. They wander past a Western street front, where we can see workers preparing a backdrop above and behind it (for the film *Copper Canyon* [1950][13]), and then come upon the permanent New York street set. 'Look at this street,' Betty says of the buildings, with fronts that have nothing behind them. 'All cardboard, all hollow, all phoney, all done with mirrors. You know, I like it better than any street in the world. Maybe because I used to play here when I was a kid.' The backlot is a hollow copy of reality (the sense of the term *verisimilitude*) and it is where the play of fantasy can run loose to be consumed by 'those wonderful people out there in the dark' (the sense in which studios were called 'dream factories'), yet in *Sunset Boulevard* it is also the actual location where the night-time scene takes place and was shot (the film's real-life set).

The self-reflexivity of the Paramount scenes makes us more conscious of the artifice behind the verisimilitude of *Sunset Boulevard* from beginning to end, which is also to say that 'it makes the fakery more realistic' (Ames 1997: 209). Cinematic realism, we are made to see, built on illusions, is the legerdemain of film-making. The large mansion used for the exterior of Norma's house was not on Sunset Boulevard but filmed at a now-demolished mansion in midtown Los Angeles, located at the intersection of Irving and Wilshire, with a swimming pool added by the studio for the filming. The interiors, however, were sets at Paramount, with Norma's second-floor bedroom constructed on stage 5 and the first floor on stage 9 (Staggs 2002: 82, 86). Wilder filmed the front of Schwab's famous drugstore at the actual site on Sunset Boulevard in West Hollywood, but scenes that take place inside were shot on a soundstage's recreation of the interior (89). Likewise, the opening shots of the Alto Nido apartments are of the real building at Franklin and Ivar in Hollywood, but the interior of Joe's cramped apartment is a set (92). And when Norma takes him shopping, the drive to the store was shot on a street in Beverly Hills, while the inside of the shop was filmed at Bullock's department store a few miles away in the mid-Wilshire district (89).

It is important, too, that Joe and Betty fall in love while working together at Paramount. With her youth and her hair that smells 'like freshly laundered handkerchiefs, like a brand-new automobile', as Joe informs her, the twenty-two-year-old Betty offers him a contrast with the more mature Norma, who smells of tube roses (a scent he dislikes) and owns an antique foreign car. Yet even though Betty has given up hopes of becoming an actress, content to work 'on the other side of the camera' where 'it's really more fun', like Norma, she is a product of Hollywood, a third-generation worker who grew up two blocks from the studio lot. Joe's collaboration with Betty on a script parallels his partnership with the older woman when he edits her screenplay. And when Betty falls in love with Joe, she will have to jilt her fiancé, Artie, just as Joe will have to find a way to leave

Norma for good. That this romance happens against the backdrop of Hollywood's manufacturing of verisimilitude suggests that Joe's falling in love with Betty may not be the realistic alternative to his imprisonment in Norma's fantasy world that he imagines.

Joe's collaboration with Betty points to an additional factor that makes *Sunset Boulevard* 'a most unusual motion picture': the male protagonist is a screenwriter, a relative rarity in backstudios prior to 1950. Actually, two backstudios with screenwriters as protagonists came out that year: Columbia's *In a Lonely Place*, starring Humphrey Bogart and directed by Nicholas Ray, opened in New York City in May, followed by the August premiere there of *Sunset Boulevard*. Both films then opened in Los Angeles on the same day, 24 August. Both, moreover, are considered film noirs. The production and release of the two pictures occurred when the status of screenwriters in Hollywood was precarious, to put it mildly.

With one or two exceptions, screenwriters during the studio era never had the standing or authority of directors. Wilder himself was an exceptional case because he and collaborator Charles Brackett had already been treated like stars at Paramount before Wilder turned to directing and Brackett to producing in order to protect their scripts; moreover, Wilder received more for co-writing *Sunset Boulevard* than he did for directing it.[14] But generally speaking, most screenwriters were seldom allowed, let alone expected, to be on set during production; and they often did not know if they had received screen credit until they saw their film as a paying customer. Not only did script revisions go through several hands before reaching a final draft, but writers were often assigned different tasks during that process, with some specialising in dialogue, characterisation or story development, while others wrote for a specific star or served as script doctors on troubled pictures once shooting had started. Joe caustically refers to how the standard practice of using a series of writers radically transformed some scripts when he mentions to Norma that his last film was about Okies in the Dust Bowl but by the time it was finished it took place on a torpedo boat. Writers were perceived as just another cog in the production-line manufacturing of motion pictures. Nor did screenwriters receive the copyright on what they created; copyright assigns authorship as the basis for conferring ownership as well as royalties, and studios owned their product. However, their status as industrial workers gave writers the legal ability to form a union under the National Labor Relations Act of 1935. Fought by the studios, the hard-won Screenwriters Guild acquired the legitimate right to strike and negotiate with the studios on behalf of its membership.

Since the Great Depression many guild members were still or had been members of the Communist Party USA or they had attended Communist Party study groups. In 1947, with the heating up of the Cold War, their leftish politics were under investigation by the House Un-American Activities Committee (HUAC) of the US Congress. Scholars have agreed that the hearings were anti-labour, given the attention paid to union leaders and agitators, and anti-Semitic, given the subpoenas to and eventual blacklisting of so many Jews, as well as being anti-Communist. Among the ten men who were called in 1947 to testify before the committee, seven were screenwriters. Billy Wilder, along with scores of other Hollywood liberals such as Humphrey Bogart, Lauren Bacall, Danny Kaye, Myrna Loy, John Huston and William Wyler, at first supported the group of subpoenaed men, agreeing with them that the committee's investigation was a direct threat to the US Constitution's guarantee of freedom of speech and thought. Forming the Committee for the First Amendment, they held several fundraising events and produced two radio spots featuring many stars to campaign against HUAC, and a plane-load of Hollywood people flew to Washington DC to attend the hearings.[15]

In DC the ten hostile witnesses refused to answer the committee's questions about their political histories and were charged with contempt of Congress. After the divisive hearings concluded, public opinion turned against that small group, immediately dubbed 'the Hollywood Ten' and 'the Unfriendly Ten'. Fearing a backlash against the film industry, the studio heads joined together and collectively announced what amounted to a blacklisting of the Ten as well as the other so-called unfriendly witnesses who had been subpoenaed by HUAC but not called to testify. The blacklisting was soon extended to everyone who did not disavow their radical pasts by confessing to party membership or flirtation and by providing the names of other party members. Hollywood liberals renounced their support of the Ten, and the Screenwriters Guild was beclouded by suspicion because of its history of radical activity. As for the Hollywood Ten, they unsuccessfully appealed their contempt convictions to the Supreme Court and began to serve their one- or two-year prison terms in 1950. And things would only get worse for Hollywood liberals and radicals as the decade unfolded.

The significance of Dixon Steele's (Humphrey Bogart) situation as a screenwriter in *In a Lonely Place* has been contextualised in those events. As James Palmer notes, 'Ostensibly a less than gripping murder mystery, the film succeeds primarily by envisioning the shared paranoia of a Hollywood community where police and friends alike suspect screenwriter Dix Steele of murdering a young woman' (1985: 200). Given the political climate, Palmer continues:

> it is not surprising that *In a Lonely Place* is not a frontal attack on the government for its political persecution of Hollywood professionals. The film ignores the national source of political repression to focus on the effects of persecution and paranoia in the personal lives of several characters. (204)

For instance, with the police having access to information from the studios, we learn that Dix has already been under surveillance throughout the past decade by virtue of the 'free exchange of information between the studios and the investigative apparatus of the state', an arrangement that suggests the writer is never fully outside the system even when unemployed (Perkins 1992: 224). Much like the files accumulated from the surveillance of people in Hollywood by the FBI, a dossier profiling Dix's violent behaviour during the 1940s supports the circumstantial evidence that he may have committed the brutal murder. The overlapping of state surveillance and personal betrayals expresses what *In a Lonely Place* does not directly call out – namely, the aftermath of HUAC in the blacklisting of many writers. Until his innocence is clarified in the final scene, ongoing suspicion of him causes Dix to act as if he were as guilty as the police presume.

Joe Gillis's situation in *Sunset Boulevard* does not parallel as neatly the postwar surveillance and blacklisting of screenwriters, but one can argue that the script uses his marginalisation in the film industry to hint at it, however obliquely. To be sure, on the surface the film-makers were uninterested in the fate of blacklisted writers. Brackett's diary records his strong disagreement with the Ten's stance on the First Amendment. DeMille and Hedda Hopper brought their public profiles to *Sunset Boulevard* and both were vociferous supporters of HUAC, the blacklist and a loyalty oath. As for Wilder, he had lent his name to the formation of the Committee for the First Amendment but did not directly participate in its activities as other signatories did. Wilder famously quipped, 'Of the Ten, two had talent and the rest were just unfriendly.' His biographer reports that 'Wilder's politics had always leaned to the left, but he was becoming even less actively so by 1947' (Sikov 1998: 274). Nonetheless, in 1947 Brackett wrote of his disagreement with Wilder about the Ten, noting, 'Billy informed me that he wasn't a communist but he gave considerably to the left, which makes him a Fellow Traveler I should think' (Slide 2015: 327). Joseph McBride, in fact, believes that their disagreement about HUAC and the subsequent blacklist 'was the issue that finally ruptured the relationship', causing the dissolution of their partnership after *Sunset Boulevard* (2021: 214).[16]

All the same, that a screenwriter as well as a has-been movie star is Hollywood's victim in *Sunset Boulevard* is worth pondering. The film mentions Joe's membership of the Screenwriters Guild twice; and to be a writer and guild member after 1947 was always to have to look over your shoulder and worry about your future. In the opening Joe mentions that he 'hadn't worked for a studio in a long time'. Although he is still 'grinding out stories, two a week', his treatments fail to attract studio interest. Before meeting Norma he admits to himself that he ought to return to his Ohio hometown and accept his inability to achieve the Hollywood dream, much as blacklisted writers would have to leave LA to find work elsewhere, stay there and write under pseudonyms or with a cleared writer's name as a front, or find jobs in other industries. Joe's voiceover, moreover, which holds the film tightly together by easing transitions from scene to scene, amounts to a confession of both his victimisation and his guilt for prostituting himself to Norma and to Hollywood – and remember that confession would become the means of clearing oneself to work in the industry. In hindsight, *Sunset Boulevard* seems eerily prescient.

Whereas in *In a Lonely Place* Hollywood's blacklist provides a structuring absence for what happens in the diegesis, in *Sunset Boulevard* it adds to the dusty atmosphere that Joe Gillis breathes. The blacklist, while not alluded to directly, nevertheless helps to amplify conditions that were already an industrial backdrop of Joe's failure to get traction as a screenwriter. That no one will hire him establishes what he will have in common with Norma when they meet, although her wealth lets her easily gain the upper hand in their relationship. She enables Joe to glimpse the Hollywood dream of success – in the expensive clothes she buys for him, the jewellery she gives him, the chauffeur-driven foreign automobile and the swimming pool he mentions that he had always wanted. 'Well, in the end he got himself a pool,' Joe sarcastically says of himself as *Sunset Boulevard* opens with the shot of his corpse in the water, '—only the price turned out to be a little high.' The irony here is typical of how Wilder's wit leavens his dark material with sly humour.

When his flashback begins Joe is desperate to retain his car because it gives him independence in automobile-happy Los Angeles. Its loss when the repo men haul it away from Norma's garage is the outward sign of his vulnerability and his emasculation by Norma. As a writer he has no standing in the industry, since he must keep deferring to the authority of those higher up in the Hollywood hierarchy; he even begs his agent and Sheldrake for loans, which each man refuses. The producer is not interested in his scripts, the agent tells him to find other management, and the ten phone calls Joe subsequently makes at Schwab's yield no loans to pay for his car or offers of employment, so he has been blacklisted in effect, if not in deed. It is no surprise that Joe warns Betty, as he sends her away from Norma's mansion, that they have no guarantee Sheldrake will ultimately want their screenplay.

Joe and Betty, moreover, bespeak different attitudes towards screenwriting. Joe may have talent, as Betty intuits, but he has become a Hollywood hack, churning out banal scripts 'from hunger', as she comments in Sheldrake's office. Betty finds in his unproduced 'Dark Windows' a six-page flashback that's 'true' and 'moving', as she tells him at Artie's New Year's Eve party, possibly because the character is based on a schoolteacher Joe once had. But he replies, 'who wants true? Who wants moving?' At the party Betty leads Joe into the bathroom where they can 'talk shop' in private, but he deflects a serious discussion by quoting movie clichés with her. As Alan Nadel points out about their repartee in this scene, 'their ability to embrace quotation with self-conscious authority nevertheless demonstrates a mutually seductive mastery of craft and industry' (2018: 71). And this seductive mastery has sexual resonance for the couple, too, since right before they are interrupted by someone telling Joe he can use the telephone, they almost kiss, making their mutual sexual attraction apparent to us if not yet consciously to them.

Still, their commitment to the craft differs. Joe is wedded to thinking in terms of familiar genres, as when he pitches his trite baseball picture to Sheldrake or explains to Betty when they meet

again in her cubicle at Paramount, 'psychopaths sell like hot cakes'. Betty, for her part, tells Joe in Sheldrake's office that 'pictures should say a little something'. By the time they run into each other at Schwab's, she has sold the producer on her idea for a 'true' and 'moving' treatment based on the teacher from 'Dark Windows' and has twenty pages of notes, but she needs more of a story, so she wants to work with Joe on developing one. 'I don't want to be a reader all my life,' she declares at Schwab's. 'I want to write.' When they meet again on the Paramount lot, she elaborates on her ideas for the script: 'This story is about teachers – their threadbare lives, their struggles. Here are people doing the most important job in the world, and they have to worry about getting enough money to re-sole their shoes. To me, it can be as exciting as any chase, any gunplay.' Yet Betty confesses that she needs Joe's help because she can't do it alone. If he wants to write popcorn pictures and she social problem films, their collaboration implies how they marry their different attitudes towards screenwriting in 'Untitled Love Story', as it says on the first page of their script.

Once he agrees to collaborate on the script, Joe has fun, he says, writing alongside Betty. Writing now reminds him of when he was twelve and snuck out of the house to see a gangster picture, as he also tells us. Their working together enables Joe to regain the pleasure in his craft that he had apparently lost by turning to hackneyed formulas like 'Bases Loaded'. His skill in thinking generically softens Betty's concern with representing 'threadbare lives' so that it will seem less radical; they are, after all, writing a love story. Insofar as *Sunset Boulevard* implies that their screenplay has merit although its future is unknown and, more to the point, that in the climax at Norma's mansion, Betty tells Joe to leave with her and that she is ignoring whatever happened between him and the faded star, we ought to ask, why doesn't he go with the young woman he loves? Instead, Joe sends Betty away. His rejection of her, his repudiation of Norma and all she has given him and his planned departure from Los Angeles morally vindicate Joe despite the numerous compromises he has made.

With that vindication in mind, and as a contrast with both Betty's insistence that films should say something about 'threadbare

lives' and Norma's bloated biblical epic, can we consider, as Nadel suggests (2018: 72), that Joe's running voiceover commentary amounts to another screenplay of sorts? Rather than delving into 'threadbare lives', this screenplay peels back the glamour and tinsel of Hollywood to reveal the industry's indifference to its past history and callous treatment of people like Norma and Joe, and for this reason one may see it as 'the honest screenplay of the sort Betty has been urging him to create' (74). And if, as Justin Gautreau claims, 'Joe's voice will live on in Betty's work' (2021: 167), it is worth noting that Joe's narration still begins with a car chase and ends in gunplay. Furthermore, if 'psychopaths sell like hotcakes', many viewers, set up by Joe's voiceover as he views the 'unhappy' house and compares it to the crazy Miss Havisham's, see Norma that same way from her first scene with Joe – the basis by which some scholars have considered *Sunset Boulevard* a classic example of film noir.

In a relatively early American book on film noir, Foster Hirsch called 'megalomaniacal' Norma 'the embodiment of Hollywood's rotting foundations, its terminal narcissism, its isolation from reality' (1981: 119). '[Her] lost fame and fading beauty', he comments, 'turn her into a psychopathic recluse' (193). Julie Grossman, however, explains that when film noirs like *Sunset Boulevard* 'portray women who seem insane', these femme fatales 'are, in narrative terms, mentally unstable, but their instability reflects a rebellion against patriarchal rules that ... make them crazy, ready to act and react violently to the authority figures and patriarchal institutions that govern their lives' (2009: 70). Despite her unbalanced mental state, Norma is not without that kind of 'crazy' agency, since she has also been called 'the most highly stylised "spider woman" in all of film noir as she weaves a web to trap and finally destroy her young victim, but even as she visually dominates him, she is presented as caught by the same false value system' (Place 1998: 53). Janey Place refers here to Swanson's domination of the film frame when she and Holden are both in the same shot. Similarly, the caption to a photo in Place's essay describes Norma's 'perverse, decaying side of film noir sexuality,

with her claw-like hands and bizarre cigarette holder' (54). Place observes in another caption, 'the attention that Norma Desmond pays to herself, as opposed to the man, is the obvious narrative transgression of *Sunset Boulevard*'(57).

If a transgressive woman gazing at her image in mirrors is a common trope in noir, then Norma magnifies this convention with the hundreds of photographs of her youth that surround her in every room, staring back at her as ideal mirror reflections. 'How could she breathe in that house, so crowded with Norma Desmonds,' Joe asks in voiceover as the camera scans thirty-some photographs on a low, wide bureau. 'More Norma Desmonds,' he adds. 'And still more Norma Desmonds.' As in many other noirs, *Sunset Boulevard* juxtaposes Norma's femme fatale with Betty's blonde good-girl. Place calls this second female figure 'the nurturing woman' who, as an 'alternative to the nightmare landscape of film noir', offers 'the alienated, lost man' the possibility of hope and stability – although usually that possibility must go unrealised for him, as happens in *Sunset Boulevard* (1998: 61).

As discussed several times already, Norma's mansion is shrouded in shadows, an effect of lighting and the *mise en scène*; due to his white shirts in the early scenes, Joe tends to be the sole bright spot. This atmosphere largely explains why Norma makes a sinister impression, as also noted already. The many photos that reflect her frozen self-image, the cigarette smoke that trails upwards to her face, the talon-like fingers that claw at the air, the narcissistic self-absorption, the defiance in her voice – these exaggerated characteristics of the femme fatales of film noir may make Norma seem like a monstrous figure of perverse sexual ambition, turning *Sunset Boulevard* into a kind of horror film.

In contrast with the daylight scenes occurring away from Sunset Boulevard, as when she visits Paramount, where her vulnerability is more apparent and a source of her pathos, Norma dominates Joe in her mansion, her lair. For here she can transform Joe into her Valentino-like lover, replacing his worn clothes with expensive tailored ones. As Gautreau puts it, 'If Max assumes the role of the leading man in Norma's mansion, Joe unwittingly takes on the role of the leading man in Norma's cinematic fantasy,' as she '[refashions] him to fit her image of early Hollywood masculinity and extravagance' (2021: 162). Norma makes this intent unmistakable on New Year's Eve when she praises the cut of Joe's tuxedo, gives him a solid gold cigarette case and leads him into a tango on a tiled dance floor inspired by Valentino. But hasn't this desire been on her mind and apparent to viewers all along? Before then, she has ordered Joe to sit down to read a portion of her script, and he obediently sits down;

has Max pay his back rent and move his things to the spare room over the garage; told Joe to spit out his chewing gum and criticised his 'dreadful shirt'; and does not care that the repo men tow away his car. Then Norma has Joe moved into the husband's bedroom adjacent to her suite.

New Year's Eve is a temporary breaking point for Joe. Drunk on champagne Norma confesses her love but he backs away, declaring she has no right to take him for granted. She replies incredulously, 'What right? Do you want me to tell you?' When her suicide attempt draws him back into her web, the couple are shot in a way that suggests Norma is like a vampire clutching her victim, ready to suck his blood (Fischer 1988: 103). By the same token, when Joe accepts his position as her toy boy, to my mind Norma becomes more sympathetic than monstrous because of her pathos: we know that her happiness in being in love with Joe and from preparing for her comeback with DeMille is delusional and will be short-lived.

Norma's domination of Joe makes him the kind of protagonist we typically find in film noir, one who thinks he can game the system

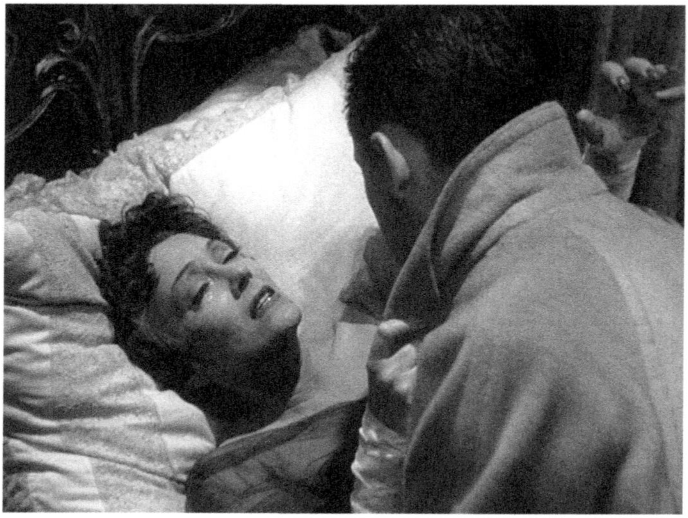

but turns out to be its victim. Joe assumes he can exploit Norma when he agrees to edit her terrible screenplay but she quickly turns the tables on him. His running voiceover, another noir convention, articulates the doomed fatality of a dead man as soon as *Sunset Boulevard* begins. That Joe is this dead man and that his voiceover mediates what happens in *Sunset Boulevard* may be enough to direct your identification with him. After all, his voiceover resists Norma's ownership of him – and her authorship of *his* story. Point-of-view shots favour Joe, unifying what we see on screen with what we hear. For instance, Joe comments about the numerous Norma Desmonds and the camera follows his gaze across the room as he scans the many photos. Joe's redemption in the climax when he sends Betty back to Artie, plans to return to Dayton, yet becomes the fatal victim of Norma's delusions may clinch one's identification with him because he gets to take the moral high ground at the last minute. Yet there is unmistakable irony in his ending, too. As Wilder told Crowe, 'it came back to that line we [the writers] had discussed for a long time. He always wanted to have a pool. He got a pool. He died in the pool. That was what we hung onto' (1999: 320).

Norma is unforgettable, a larger-than-life figure, so she yields different and complex responses from viewers; as a result, the film repeatedly fractures and challenges one's affinity with Joe. After all, he is surprised when Norma confesses her love on New Year's Eve, which indicates that, even though he is narrating the film after the fact, he was not paying close enough attention to her behaviour, as an alert viewer does, for he was blinded by his second-rate hustling. Similarly, since he is shocked at Max's revelation in the garage about his history with Norma, Joe must not have been listening in the earlier scene when the butler pointed out what had been his former, lavishly appointed office as a director on the Paramount lot. For that matter, Joe's prostitution as Norma's kept man even before her suicide attempt – recall that on New Year's Eve she asks but does not need to spell out why she has the right to do with Joe as she pleases – serves as a metaphor for the familiar 'writer-as-prostitute' conceit

(Ames 1997: 210). This stereotype makes Joe morally ambiguous as a protagonist and narrator, even with his redemption; as a writer for hire, whether by a movie studio or an older woman, his choices suggest how, like other noir heroes, he is caught up in the darkness of the corrupt world he inhabits. In other film noirs that corruption arises from gangsters, gamblers, dirty cops or rich, powerful men; in *Sunset Boulevard* it arises from Hollywood, which draws young hopefuls like Joe Gillis from the Midwest to Los Angeles, only to toss them aside when they cease to matter.

Norma's monstrousness as the deadly spider woman of film noir begs the question of who is to blame for what happens in that musty old mansion on Sunset Boulevard. The ending of *Sunset Boulevard* shows how easily Hollywood can discount its responsibility for Norma's plight, allowing the press to personalise her shooting Joe as a 'crime of passion' by a 'forgotten star' who is insane. Yet once upon a time in Hollywood, *Sunset Boulevard* asks us to remember, stars like Norma *were* larger than life, filling the screen with their glorious, glamorous and silent faces for 'those wonderful people out there in the dark'. When Norma whispers that stars never age, she only gets it half-right: biologically, stars do decay but as images they remain ageless on celluloid and in photographs. As Joe comments to Norma early on, 'You *used* to be big,' implying that she has now shrunk in stature and importance. She replies defiantly, 'it's the pictures that got small.' But it is also those numerous pictures that surround her in her mansion, like the old movies that still enchant her, which forever will remain larger than her life.

4 After *Sunset Boulevard*

Billy Wilder was considered to be at the top of his game with *Sunset Boulevard*. It 'brings with it no sweetness, light, or customary glamour,' stated the review in the *Los Angeles Times*. 'But it is an enormously fascinating film, and will undoubtedly bid high for Academy Award attention' (Schallert 1950). As awards season rolled around, *Sunset Boulevard* found a worthy competitor in *All About Eve* (1950), Joseph L. Mankiewicz's drama about an ageing Broadway actress played by Bette Davis in what became a signature role for her. The two films were a fitting match-up, with Wilder's holding a mirror up to Hollywood and Mankiewicz's doing the same to the cut-throat world of theatre. After their respective downtown openings, the pair made for a smart double bill in second-run theatres in some cities as well. Although Swanson was ten years older than Davis and the latter had only recently left Warner Bros., both films were received as triumphant comeback vehicles for their stars. Both films also confirmed their directors' talents: Mankiewicz had won

Chicago Tribune, 17 November 1950, Part 3, p. 15

Oscars for writing and directing the year before for *A Letter to Three Wives* (1949) and Wilder had won in the same categories for *The Lost Weekend*.

When the Academy Award nominations were announced on 12 February 1951, the two films were almost neck and neck, *All About Eve*'s fourteen nominations just topping *Sunset Boulevard*'s eleven. Prior to the awards ceremony, *Sunset Boulevard* had taken the Best Picture and Actress prizes from the National Board of Review, while *All About Eve* had won those two categories as well as the one for directing from the New York Film Critics Circle. At the Golden Globes *Sunset Boulevard* took the honours for picture (drama), directing, actress and musical score. *All About Eve* won for screenwriting. The Screenwriters Guild split the difference, with *All About Eve* winning for Best Written American Comedy and *Sunset Boulevard* for Best Written American Drama.

At the Oscars, which took place simultaneously in Hollywood and New York City on 29 March, anticipation was high. *All About Eve* got the glory, winning six, including ones for picture, directing and adapted screenplay; but the night's big suspense was who would win for Best Actress, Swanson or Davis? Many felt that Davis's chances had been hurt by co-star Anne Baxter (who played the manipulative Eve) running against her in the same category. In her memoir Swanson quotes the numerous newspaper columns that predicted her to win over Davis (1980: 249–52). When the Best Actress winner was named, it appeared that Swanson and Davis may have cancelled each other out, since the award surprisingly went to a newcomer, Judy Holliday, who repeated her star-making Broadway role in *Born Yesterday* (1950), a comedy also starring William Holden. Swanson recalled being unmoved about losing. 'I hadn't thought I would be greatly affected one way or another, and I wasn't. I knew Hollywood too well' (258). Possibly because the category was not in direct competition with *All About Eve*, Wilder did go home with the award for original screenplay, which he shared with Brackett and Marshman.

One, Two, Three (1961)

Wilder's momentum at Paramount abruptly screeched to a halt with his next film, *Ace in the Hole* (1951), a cynical exposé of ruthless, opportunistic journalism. After its poor initial openings in the summer, the studio renamed it *The Big Carnival*, but the title change did not help. Wilder rebounded with *Stalag 17* (1953) and *Sabrina* (1954), which began a string of mostly hits during the rest of the decade that reached their peak with *Some Like it Hot* (1959) and *The Apartment* (1960). Wilder considered *The Apartment*, which garnered him Academy Awards for producing, directing and writing, his most perfectly realised film. By 1959, Wilder's name on a poster had become an advertising brand, as much of a draw as a star's. For *One, Two, Three* (1961) his full-length photograph, and not star James Cagney's, was used in the ad art.

With *Love in the Afternoon* (1957), considered an homage to his idol Ernst Lubitsch, Wilder had found a new writing partner in I. A. L. Diamond. The two men formed a happy collaborative team for the rest of Wilder's career that rivalled 'brackettandwilder', ending only with Diamond's death shortly before Wilder himself retired. Angry at the studio's handling of his POW comedy *Stalag 17* in Germany, Wilder had departed Paramount following the release of *Sabrina* and worked independently until signing with the Mirisch Company and United Artists for *Some Like it Hot*; thereafter and with basically a free hand, he and Diamond (eventually promoted to an associate producer as well as co-writer) made films for Mirisch and UA until they moved to Universal for *The Front Page* (1974).

Wilder had always been a director who worked well with and understood how to use stars: Marlene Dietrich in *A Foreign Affair* (1948) and *Witness for the Prosecution* (1957); Audrey Hepburn in *Sabrina* and *Love in the Afternoon*; Marilyn Monroe in *The Seven Year Itch* and *Some Like it Hot*; and William Holden in *Stalag 17* and *Sabrina*, as well as *Sunset Boulevard* and *Fedora* (1978). Jack Lemmon, who starred in *Some Like it Hot* and *The Apartment*, became a Wilder favourite. The actor went on to perform in five more films for the director.

Wilder had his most financially successfully film with *Irma La Douce* (1963), which paired Lemmon and Shirley MacLaine, his co-star from *The Apartment*, but he stumbled the next year with another sex farce, the controversial *Kiss Me, Stupid* (1964). This film had Dean Martin playing a cartoonish version of his persona and Kim Novak in a role originally written for Monroe. Condemned by the Catholic Legion of Decency and for that reason released by a UA subsidiary, *Kiss Me, Stupid* instigated a critical backlash against the director. Although Wilder had in the past skewered bourgeois sexual mores in his films, and *Sunset Boulevard* was itself cutting edge for Hollywood in 1950 with its tale of a fifty-year-old woman's sexual relationship with a man half her age, critics declared that *Kiss Me, Stupid* set a new low for Wilder due to its cynicism, smirking sexual jokes and overall vulgarity. Although his name still had purchase, Wilder's currency as far as the industry was concerned never fully regained its previous high ground after *Kiss Me, Stupid*, which is also to say that his wit and biting sarcasm failed to keep up with the rapid changes in American culture characterising the revolutionary 1960s and early 70s. Nonetheless, his best films – and *Sunset Boulevard* is at the top of the list alongside *Double Indemnity*, *The Lost Weekend*, *Some Like it Hot* and *The Apartment* – have always confirmed Wilder's reputation as one of the studio era's greatest and most imaginative writer-directors.

Wilder's former partner at Paramount, Charles Brackett, left that studio immediately after *Sunset Boulevard*, signing on as a producer and sometimes writer at Twentieth Century-Fox. Like Wilder, Brackett had a string of successes in the 1950s, although with some exceptions, such as *Niagara* (1953) and *The King and I* (1956), most were middlebrow comedies and melodramas. Brackett won another Oscar in 1953 for co-writing *Titanic* and an honorary one in 1958. The two men apparently did not maintain contact with each other but they did meet in public once more when they were sued for plagiarising *Sunset Boulevard* by a former Paramount accountant in October 1951, a groundless charge that was officially settled in their favour after two and a half years; a second, separate, plagiarism charge was filed against them in 1954 but thrown out by the court a year later (Sikov 1998: 310–11). Respectful of each other's talent and courteous towards each other to the end, Wilder and Brackett were reticent to discuss their breakup in the press, although Wilder spoke out publicly about his anger at Fox's mistreatment of his former partner when the studio, at that point in deep financial trouble, let Brackett go in 1962, forcing him into retirement, ostensibly due to his ill health.

Sunset Boulevard and Wilder were instrumental in making William Holden one of the biggest stars of the postwar era. After *Sunset Boulevard*, Holden and Nancy Olson were considered a romantic team, co-starring in three more films: *Union Station* (1950), *Force of Arms* (1951) and *Submarine Command* (1951). None were very remarkable, and like his role in *Born Yesterday*, they reiterated what Holden liked to call his 'Smiling Jim' screen image: handsome, charming and muscular but also decent and ordinary. *Sunset Boulevard* revealed a dark side to that image, given the opportunism and sexuality driving Joe Gillis, and Wilder's *Stalag 17*, which won Holden the Best Actor Oscar that had eluded him for *Sunset Boulevard*, and *Sabrina* (to a lesser extent) reiterated it. By 1956 Holden ranked first in a *Motion Picture Herald* poll of top stars, and *Photoplay* named him their star of the year for both 1955 and 1956. Although his heteronormality as a leading man was never in question, melodramas like *The Country Girl* (1954), *Love Is a Many-Splendored Thing* (1955), *Picnic* (1955) and

The Proud and the Profane (1956) revealed the possibly dangerous yet undeniably exciting sexuality underlying his 'Smiling Jim' image. While he remained an A-list leading man until the end of his life, off screen Holden was a heavy drinker. His unexpected passing in 1981 happened when, alone in his home, he fell while drunk, hit his head, became unconscious and bled to death.

Gloria Swanson was so closely identified with Norma Desmond that as far as the public was concerned the two identities were interchangeable. True, Swanson had not made a picture for almost a decade but she had made a few talkies, and she was active in New York on the stage, radio and television before returning to Hollywood for Wilder's film in 1949. But after her bravura performance in *Sunset Boulevard*, the ghost of Norma haunted Swanson for the rest of her life, however much she tried to shake free of the character.

In advance of its opening late in the summer, early in 1950 Paramount sent Swanson on a cross-country tour of thirty-three cities in thirty weeks to promote her return to the screen (Staggs 2002: 186). During the film's production, newspaper articles recounted her career in silent films yet focused on her comeback. A feature story in the *New York Times*, for instance, compared her return to pictures to what was known at the time about the character she was playing, all the while describing Swanson's ever-present glamour and determination never to retire (Colton 1949).

Swanson, moreover, appeared to enjoy the praise heaped on her for her daring performance. After *Sunset Boulevard* opened, she returned to New York and at the end of 1950 co-starred with José Ferrer in a Broadway revival of *Twentieth Century*; she starred in another play the following year. She had a leading role in one more film, *3 for Bedroom C* (1952). Realising that the parts now being offered to her were all variations of the crazed faded movie star, Swanson decided:

> I didn't want to spend the rest of my life, until I couldn't remember lines any more or read cue cards, playing Norma Desmond over and over again.

And if serious producers and directors were foolish enough to think that was the only role I could play and get box-office returns, then it was time to look around this highly diversified world and find some other things to do before I died. (Swanson 1980: 489)

Thereafter, although she did an occasional cameo in films, she appeared mostly in guest roles on television while engaging in her other interests, such as her fashion line, painting and sculpture, and health foods. All the same, she could not elude Norma even on television. For instance, in December 1961 she made a guest appearance in an ABC adventure series, *Straightaway*, in which she played 'A glamorous movie queen of a past era, suspected of being a hit-and run-driver' (Hoffman 1961: 8).

Despite her denials, Swanson herself never appeared able to let Norma go entirely. In 1953 she hired Dickson Hughes and Richard Stapley, a gay couple, to write the score for a musical version of *Sunset Boulevard*, now called 'Boulevard!' In 1957 she performed one number – Norma's first song, drawn from her penultimate line in the film and entitled 'Wonderful People' – on Steve Allen's television show. While Swanson thought Paramount had given her the rights to pursue the musical's development, enabling her to begin negotiating with producers and possible directors, the studio ultimately stopped the project after she had worked on it for several years by refusing to grant her permission to use the property. A new documentary, *Boulevard! A Hollywood Story*, gives an account of the project and its backstage drama; for much like Norma, as well as behaving in high diva mode, Swanson allegedly became infatuated with Stapley, who resisted her overtures, and the resulting tension eventually caused his departure, ending his relationship with Hughes. Hughes later repurposed the score in December 1994 as a Hollywood nightclub show about the musical's creation, *Swanson on Sunset* (*Boulevard!* 2021; see also Rich 1994; Staggs 2002: 202–23).

For all the film's accolades in the US and abroad, Staggs comments, 'Worldwide acclaim, however, could not save *Sunset*

Boulevard from a long period of obscurity.' Following the usual pattern for studio product in the US (downtown first-runs, second- and third-runs in neighbourhood houses, smaller venues in suburban and rural areas, double or triple bills at drive-ins), 'it disappeared' (2002: 188). It would be ten years before *Sunset Boulevard* reappeared at revival houses like the New Yorker cinema on upper Broadway in Manhattan or museums like Chicago's Art Institute, where it renewed interest among cinephiles and critics.

Still, *Sunset Boulevard* was never entirely gone from public consciousness in the 1950s because of radio and television adaptations. Swanson and Holden repeated their roles in an hour-long abridgement on *Radio Theater* on 17 September 1951, and it was broadcast twice on NBC television in the hour format, first on *Lux Video Theater* on 6 January 1955 with Miriam Hopkins (as Norma) and James Daly (Joe) and again on 3 December 1956 on *Robert Montgomery Presents* with Mary Astor (Norma) and Darren McGavin (Joe).

I have had a chance to see a kinescope of the 1956 adaptation. This version faithfully follows the storyline, albeit in a quick-paced, condensed form so that while this *Sunset Boulevard* ticks off almost all the film's plot points, everything happens abruptly. DeMille is omitted, replaced by Sheldrake, who is now a famous long-time director as well as a producer, but Joe's voiceover remains, albeit cut back, and some of that commentary is handed over to Montgomery, who introduces each of the show's three acts. This version even lets us glimpse a fragment of silent film featuring a young Mary Astor. Although some expense went into the sets – the exterior of Norma's house has a real swimming pool, and Joe's body is seen floating in it at the opening just as he falls into it when she shoots him – the problem lies in the acting as well as the rapid pacing of the story.

With the exception of Astor, an old hand from her decades in films, the others speak dialogue quickly and often bark (or in McGavin's case, sometimes growl) their lines; speed of delivery aside, there is no apparent difference between McGavin's and Astor's performance styles. Astor started acting in shorts in 1921, moving on to leads during that decade, but she saw her career soar in talkies during the 1930s, culminating in her femme fatale in *The Maltese Falcon* (1941) and her Oscar for *The Great Lie* (1941). She uses her considerable skill to show Norma's various emotional beats but does so in the more restrained style of sound-era acting. Thus the subtlety with which Swanson's and Holden's performances differentiate old from new Hollywood regrettably got lost for a television audience. Furthermore, a dramatisation of Norma's return to Paramount is sorely missed; and Astor's declaring at the end of the hour, 'All right, Mr Sheldrake, I am ready for my close-up,' just doesn't register with the same impact of Swanson's famous final line.

The years immediately following the release of *Sunset Boulevard* also saw backstudio dramas that were clearly influenced by Norma and the jaundiced view of Hollywood informing the Billy Wilder film, such as *Hollywood Story* (1951), *The Bad and the Beautiful* (1952), *The Star* (1952), *A Star Is Born* (1954), *The Barefoot Contessa* (1954), *The Female Animal* (1958) and *The Goddess* (1958). The madwoman cloistered in her derelict-looking mansion, as well as the fifty-year-old former movie star playing her, gave rise in the 1960s to the cycle of Grand Guignol horror films starring actresses past their prime according to Hollywood's ageism, beginning with Bette Davis and Joan Crawford in *What Ever Happened to Baby Jane?* (1962). *Sunset Boulevard* itself showed up on television at around the same time. On 1 December 1963, to mark the fiftieth anniversary of Hollywood film production, NBC telecast *The World's Greatest Showman: The Legend of Cecil B. DeMille*, which, along with many major stars of his films like Swanson, featured 'full segments from the greatest DeMille epics', including his 'great performance in Sunset Boulevard [*sic*]' (*Chicago Tribune* advertisement 1963). In 1964 Paramount sold *Sunset Boulevard* as part of a package of the studio's 1950s films to the NBC network for its prime-time movie series during the 1964–5 season. After that, the package was syndicated for late-night showings.

Talk in entertainment circles about musicalising *Sunset Boulevard* continued without Swanson's participation for several decades. At one point Stephen Sondheim and Harold Prince were working on it as a vehicle for Angela Lansbury. When Sondheim mentioned the plan to Wilder, the latter told him that the film could not be made into a musical – because 'it has to be an opera. After all, it's about a dethroned queen' (Sikov 1998: 468). Ultimately, when *Sunset Boulevard* became an Andrew Lloyd Webber musical in 1993–4, it did morph into an opera of sorts as a stage vehicle for mature divas. The production was as famous for the firing of its stars as for its casting. Patti LuPone opened the show in London and was contractually guaranteed the Broadway company; however, Glenn Close, who led the Los Angeles version, was given the New York spot and LuPone was effectively let go, with Faye Dunaway hired to replace Close in LA. When Dunaway was fired before she even opened, that company was shut down. Both LuPone and Dunaway subsequently sued.

Wilder's comment that *Sunset Boulevard* 'is about a dethroned queen' was on the mark insofar as the iconic figure of the crazy movie star is probably known to many people today even if they have never seen the film. As Crowe told Wilder, 'Norma Desmond is more famous than most famous actors' (1999: 303). Norma has been celebrated while being parodied on variety and comedy series on television. The stage musical and its cast albums have certainly helped to sustain Norma's fame, and Close has been determined to play Norma in a film adaptation of the musical. In Wilder's film, though, the character of Norma is inseparable from a viewer's knowledge of the parallel past in silents that Swanson brought to the part, a dimension that now can never be duplicated.

The creation of academic programmes in film studies that begin in the 1970s and proliferated in subsequent decades further revived serious interest in *Sunset Boulevard* as a Hollywood classic and touchstone of film noir. It is still an assigned text in many film courses. Also keeping alive its status as a landmark of 1950s cinema and a crucial work in Wilder's filmography was the director's penultimate feature, *Fedora*, which he and Diamond adapted from a novella in Tom Tryon's *Crowned Heads*. According to Gerd Gemünden, the two films are companion pieces, each 'exploring questions of visibility and invisibility, the changing roles of actor, writer, and producer; the transitory experience of fame and stardom; and the merciless process of aging' (2008: 77). The films' comparability was immediately noted due to William Holden's starring role (as Barry Detweiler) and voiceover. *Fedora* inverts the premise of *Sunset Boulevard*, however. Whereas Norma is invisible to present-day Hollywood in 1950, she remains a palpable presence, just as the materiality of her star image, that gallery of her photographs, can be seen everywhere one looks in her mansion. Fedora, by contrast, turns out to be an empty mask, which raises serious doubts about the palpability of stardom.

At some time in the late 1950s, Polish-born Fedora (Marthe Keller as the young Fedora in flashbacks, Hildegard Knef as the older Fedora), a big star in Hollywood during the studio era, went too far in her efforts to reverse the ageing process with experimental but dubious surgical treatments performed by her physician, Dr Vando (José Ferrer). With her face terribly scarred by an infection and her body crippled by a stroke following the procedure, Fedora quit the movies, retreating to a secluded, fenced villa on a small Greek island. She lives there as the Countess Sobryanski, having assumed the identity of the deceased mother of her former lover, who is the father of her illegitimate daughter, Antonia (also Marthe Keller). Unexpectedly, an honorary Oscar revives Fedora's career but not in the way this award typically does. Seeing how easily the daughter, posing as her mother, fools the president of the Academy into thinking she is Fedora when he arrives at the villa to present the statuette, mother and daughter conspire to let the world think that Fedora has returned to the screen with her beauty intact. The ironic twist to their scheme is that, instead of concealing or denying her age as female stars have to do in comparison with actors like the wrinkled sixty-year-old Holden – weather-beaten, gruff-voiced and alcohol-fuelled – Antonia must look and pretend to be *older* than she really is.

William Holden as Barry Detweiler in *Fedora* (1978)

For Antonia the ruse at first serves to bring her closer to her mother, who had abandoned her during her childhood for Hollywood. For the older woman, who had removed the villa's sixty-three mirrors, the daughter becomes her looking glass. 'You must not forget who you are … You are Fedora,' Antonia is continually reminded by her caretaker, her mother's assistant, Miss Balfour (Frances Sternhagen). But as Antonia successfully takes her mother's place on screen, she becomes a highly disturbed reflection. For after years of sacrificing her own identity in order to maintain the Fedora myth, Antonia becomes infatuated with the real-life Michael York, her leading man in her latest picture, saying she plans to tell him the truth after filming is completed. Forcibly taken away by Balfour before the movie can be finished in order to preserve the illusion of Fedora at any cost, a mentally unstable Antonia becomes addicted to drugs, requiring constant supervision, straps to secure her to her bed at night and a straitjacket after she shows up in Detweiler's hotel room with her mother's love letters to sell. Then, driven to despair when Fedora's entourage, Balfour and Vando, have her locked up in hospital to keep her from contacting York, Antonia ends her life by imitating the conclusion of *Anna Karenina*, the script Detweiler wants to produce with Fedora in the starring role.

In contrast with *Sunset Boulevard*, blame for what happens to the younger woman falls squarely on the vanity and egoism of Fedora, not on Hollywood or its ageism. True, the original Fedora is, like Norma, a victim of stardom as an institution but, unlike Norma, she is a sane and unrepentant victimiser of her daughter. 'I took nothing,' Fedora claims, when Detweiler accuses her. 'I gave her everything. I made her Fedora.' The identity of 'Fedora', it turns out, is detachable, able to move from mother to daughter effortlessly. Fedora, moreover, views it as a gift bestowed upon her daughter. But Antonia, the mother declares, was 'too soft, too weak, too sentimental' to appreciate that legacy. The daughter was nevertheless strong enough to throw herself in front of a train, intentionally destroying her mother's 'face' for a second time and ending the myth of Fedora for good.

Fedora views Antonia as an alter ego, a persona she can inhabit remotely and watch perform in her name. Fedora even orchestrates her daughter's funeral as a piece of spectacular theatre, attended by hundreds of Fedora's fans. She oversees the event to the last detail and with her entourage witnesses it from a balcony. 'You sure know how to throw yourself a funeral,' Detweiler wryly observes. 'Endings are very important,' Fedora tells him, her speech reminiscent of the ending of *Sunset Boulevard*. 'That's what people remember. The last exit. The final close-up.' 'Even if you have to use a stand-in,' he replies. 'The legend must go on,' she responds. 'You've been around this business long enough. You know it's all special effects, painted backdrops, glycerine tears.' 'Magic time,' he says.

Wilder, who made *Fedora* in Europe with German financing after Universal pulled out of the project, complained about Hollywood at the end of the 1970s: 'Now the picturemaker wastes ninety percent of his energy getting the financing,' he told interviewers after *Fedora*

Fedora: Antonia's funeral, where Detweiler learns the truth was shown at Cannes (McBride and McCarthy 1979: 44). Detweiler, who travels to Greece to coax the reclusive Fedora out of retirement, a condition for him to obtain financing for his new film, is a sad Wilder surrogate, personifying an outmoded Hollywood system that once relied on stars like Fedora – and directors like Wilder. 'The kids with beards have taken over,' Detweiler grumbles to the woman he assumes is the Countess Sobryanski when pitching his screenplay, and now you 'don't need scripts, just give 'em a hand-held camera with a zoom lens'.

Fedora's charade manifests these same new industrial conditions. When she reveals the truth to Detweiler at Antonia's funeral, she explains that Fedora's 'return' was orchestrated in the 1960s via costume spectacles made in Europe, but, significantly, never in Hollywood. This detail is telling, especially if one recalls the state of American film-making in the 1960s when studio production was uncertain and reduced, and then in the 1970s when tentpole blockbusters began their domination and a new generation of young film-makers emerged. Instead, an older mythology of glamorous stardom, still operating then for some international productions, enables Fedora to rationalise her deception. 'People were tired of what passes as entertainment these days,' she reasons, obviously alluding to American filmgoing at that time. '*Cinéma vérité*. The naked truth. The uglier the better. They wanted glamour again. And who was I to disappoint them?' Wilder himself waxed nostalgic for that older star system and its glamour. Referring to the homely look of major actors in the 1970s, the director recognised that they 'can act rings around the old leading men, the handsome ones. But I'm kind of an old-fashioned romantic, you know. I like handsome people' (McBride and McCarthy 1979: 47).

Now flash-forward to 2020 and the seventieth anniversary of *Sunset Boulevard*. An article in *The Guardian* online explores why 'Sunset Boulevard [*sic*] became a landmark statement on the perils of celebrity culture'. Its thesis, that 'the film is no longer just an indictment of Hollywood's vanity but of a whole cultural ethos that values being seen', applies more to *Fedora* than to the earlier picture –

which is to say that the writer, Tom Joudrey, views *Sunset Boulevard* through the mythology of stardom motivating that later film. Declaring that *Sunset Boulevard* dramatises 'the damage wrought by fame' and the cultural imperative of 'being seen' regardless of the cost, Joudrey concludes that Norma Desmond anticipates Princess Diana, Michael Jackson, Lindsay Lohan, Taylor Swift and YouTube stars. But I don't think Norma *needs* to be seen, as he maintains; rather, Norma needs to be worshipped again on screen as her younger self. It is the impossibility of that desire that damages Norma more than the unquenchable need to be visible in public again, even in the form of a stand-in, which is what drives the reclusive Fedora.

All the same, the *Guardian* article reflects how, seven decades after its release, *Sunset Boulevard* is itself still visible because of its ability to be recontextualised in – or repurposed for – the present moment. As I noted at the start, its quotable lines have become an indelible part of our speech. How many times have people – on film or TV, in print or in person – said they were now ready for their close-up? Memes with images from *Sunset Boulevard* and lines of dialogue as captions are circulated in social media for a variety of circumstances, from birthday greetings to jokes to political comments. On the other hand, *Sunset Boulevard* still resonates forcefully for cinephiles and academics; after seventy years, it is still being analysed by amateur critics in blogs and on web pages and by professional scholars like myself in this book. The seriousness with which Wilder and company took a hard look at Hollywood still speaks profoundly, although not in the same way for everybody: some viewers, identifying with Joe perhaps, want to make it in the film industry; others, whether in an audience or as impersonators, take camp pleasure from Norma's extravagant posturing or her transgressiveness; others enjoy the insider's view of the workings of Hollywood or become enrapt by the film's haunting, noirish *mise en scène*. Above all else, *Sunset Boulevard* remains a testament to the power of film to engage and move viewers. Regardless of how you may connect to it yourself, we all continue to be 'those wonderful people out there in the dark'.

Notes

1 McBride and McCarthy 1979: 42.
2 Before going any further, I should point out my slight uncertainty about the film's title. The opening title card, the Internet Movie Database and McBride's biographical-critical study of Wilder use the abbreviation '*Sunset Blvd.*'. But the typescript of the 21 March 1949 screenplay with some revised pages (Wilder 1999), the PCA file, and the trailer and advertising spell out the street name, calling the film '*Sunset Boulevard*'. So do Wikipedia, the Zolotow, Sikov and Chandler biographies of Wilder, Crowe's book-length interview and most academic scholarship. Which to use? Assuming that the typescript of the screenplay indicated the writers' intention and that the title card uses the abbreviation because Wilder wanted the shot of the kerb for a realistic effect, I have decided to spell out 'Boulevard' throughout. But feel free to substitute the abbreviation in your mind every time I mention the title in the following pages.
3 My account of Wilder's and Brackett's biographies and working relationship is a composite of information drawn from Barnett 1944, Koury 1948, Zolotow 1996, Sikov 1998, Staggs 2002, Chandler 2002, Slide 2015 and McBride 2021.
4 According to Slide, participants in The Word Game each had a card, 'ruled into twenty-five squares, five across and five down, and placed letters in his squares as they were called out'. Whoever had the most words of five, four and three letters won; and they played for twenty-five cents a game (2015: 404). According to Barnett, they played for fifty cents a game (1944: 112). And according to Zolotow, 'Wilder always won. *Always*' (1996: 71).
5 For a brief but excellent account of Swanson's career in silents, see Desjardins 2010: 110–21.
6 For her account, see Swanson 1980: 368–75.
7 McBride discusses Lubitsch's influence on Wilder, which taught him 'how to express feelings in pictures as in words'. Nonetheless, he also notes that 'Wilder was more explicit in his narrative style than Lubitsch' (2021: 229).
8 Sam Staggs comments that the sequence in *Sunset Boulevard* anticipates the voyeuristic opening of Alfred Hitchcock's *Psycho* (1960) a decade later, which is shot similarly, but also wonders who invented 'this through-the-window shot', since it was already apparent in some of Hitchcock's early British films (2002: 92).
9 On the backstudio genre from the silent era to the present century, see Cohan 2019; on the star narrative as a subgenre, see McNally 2021.
10 Wilder has said he loved both films (McBride and McCarthy 1979: 41; Staggs 2002: 17).
11 Various scholars have discussed how the acting styles of Swanson and Holden differentiate old from new Hollywood. See Trowbridge 2002, Taylor 2007, Gemünden 2008 and Peberdy 2013. Patrice Petro, however, believes that in stylising this difference, Wilder disregarded the subtlety and sophistication of silent film acting (2010: 3).

12 'Hog-Eye' was apparently the nickname of a real person, John Hetman, a former Paramount electrician (Sikov 1998: 290).
13 Gautreau identifies the title of the film being prepared on the backlot in this scene (2021: 165).
14 Wilder received $211,416 for co-writing *Sunset Boulevard* but only $90,000 for directing (Staggs 2002: 25).
15 The political history of Hollywood before and during the HUAC hearings and the blacklist era has been well researched. I have found these books most helpful: Ceplar and Englund 1979, Navasky [1980] 1991, Buhle and Wagner 2002, Gladchuk 2007, and, for a full account of the hearings, Doherty 2018.
16 McBride discusses Wilder's opposition to the hearings and the blacklist in some detail (2021: 430–8).

Credits

Sunset Blvd.
USA
1950

Directed by
Billy Wilder
Produced by
Charles Brackett
Written by
Charles Brackett
Billy Wilder
D. M. Marshman Jr
Production Company
Paramount Pictures

Director of Photography
John F. Seitz
Art Direction
Hans Dreier
John Meehan
Special Photographic Effects
Gordon Jennings
Process Photography
Farciot Edouart
Set Decoration
Sam Comer
Ray Moyer
Editorial Supervision
Doane Harrison
Costumes
Edith Head
Edited by
Arthur Schmidt
Make-up Supervision
Wally Westmore
Sound Recording
Harry Lindgren
John Cope
Assistant Director
C. C. Coleman Jr
Music Score
Franz Waxman

uncredited
Production Manager
Hugh Brown
2nd Assistant Director
Gerd Oswald
Script Clerk
Lupe Hall
Camera Operator
Otto Pierce
Camera Assistant
Harlow Stengel
Gaffer
Walter Taylor
Grip
Fred True
Stills
Glen E. Richardson
Assistant Editor
Frank Bracht
Props
Tom Plews
Props Assistant
Jack Golconda
Wardrobe
Ed Fitzharris
Hazel Hegarty
Costume Jeweller
Joan Joseff
Make-up Artists
Frank Thayer
Karl Silvera
Hairdressers
Nellie Manley
Vera Tomei
Technical Advisor
Norris Stensland
Dialogue Coach
A. Ronald Lubin
Head Carpenter
Steve Beers
Construction Coordinator
Gene Lauritzen
Orchestrators
Sidney Cutner
George Parrish
Leonid Raab
Leo Shuken

CAST
William Holden
Joe C. Gillis
Gloria Swanson
Norma Desmond
Erich von Stroheim
Max Von Mayerling
Nancy Olson
Betty Schaefer
Fred Clark
Sheldrake
Lloyd Gough
Morino
Jack Webb
Artie Green
Franklyn Farnum
undertaker/courtier
Larry Blake
1st finance man
Charles Dayton
2nd finance man
Cecil B. DeMille
Hedda Hopper
Buster Keaton
Anna Q. Nilsson
H. B. Warner
Ray Evans
Jay Livingston
as themselves

uncredited
Roy Thompson
Rudy, shoeshine boy
Ruth Clifford
Sheldrake's secretary

Peter Drynan
tailor
Kenneth Gibson
salesman
Archie Twitchell
vicuña salesman
E. Mason Hopper
doctor/courtier
John Cortay
young Paramount gateman
Robert Emmett O'Connor
Jonesy, old Paramount gateman
Stan Johnson
Bill Sheehan
assistant directors
John 'Skins' Miller
Hog-Eye, electrician
Bert Moorhouse
Gordon Cole
Julia Faye
Hisham
Virginia Randolph
Gertrude Astor
Frank O'Connor
Eva Novak
courtiers
Ralph Montgomery
Joel Allen
prop men
Gertrude Messinger
hairdresser
Gerry Ganzer
Connie
Howard Negley
police captain
Kenneth Christy
homicide captain
Len Hendry
police sergeant
Sidney Skolsky
as himself

Eddie Dew
assistant coroner
Yvette Vickers [Vedder]
girl on telephone
Al Ferguson
phone standby
Bernice Mosk
as herself
Tommy Ivo
boy
Emmett Smith
black man
Jay Morley
fat man
Arthur A. Lane
Archie R. Dalzell
camera operators
James Hawley
Edward Wahrman
camera assistants
Sanford E. Greenwald
newsreel cameraman
Howard Joslin
police lieutenant/body in pool
Fred Aldrich
detective
Anne Bauchens
editor
Edward Biby
restaurant patron
Danny Borzage
accordionist
Rudy Germane
detective
Chuck Hamilton
grip on DeMille set
Tiny Jones
woman outside Paramount gate
Perc Launders
violinist at New Year's Eve party

Alan Marston
reporter
William Meader
Jack Warden
party guests
Harold Miller
man on golf course
Lee Miller
party guest/Paramount Studio employee
Jack Perrin
detective
Henry Wilcoxon
actor on set of DeMille's 'Samson & Delilah'
Ottola Nesmith
Joe Gray
Creighton Hale
uncredited roles

Production Details
Filmed between 11 April and 18 June 1949 (with additional scenes/retakes in late June/July 1949 and January 1950) in Beverly Hills and Los Angeles, CA.
35mm
1.37:1
Black and white
Running time: 110 minutes
Length: 9,951 feet
MPAA certification no. 13955

Release Details
US premiere on 10 August 1950 in New York; US theatrical release 1950 by Paramount Pictures
UK premiere on 17 August 1950 in London; UK theatrical release 1950 by Paramount British Pictures

Bibliography

Agee, James (1950), 'Films of the Month: *Sunset Boulevard*', *Monthly Film Bulletin*, November, pp. 283–5.

American Film Institute ([1976] 2001), 'Dialogue on Film: Billy Wilder and I. A. L. Diamond', in Robert Horton (ed.), *Billy Wilder Interviews* (Jackson: University Press of Mississippi), pp. 110–31.

Ames, Christopher (1997), *Movies About the Movies: Hollywood Reflected* (Lexington: University Press of Kentucky).

Barnett, Lincoln (1944), 'The Happiest Couple in Hollywood: Brackett & Wilder Are Movies' No. 1 Writing Team', *Life*, 21 December, pp. 101–4, 106, 110–22.

Boulevard! A Hollywood Story (2021), [Film] Dir. Jeffrey Schwarz, USA: Automat Pictures.

Buhle, Paul and Dave Wagner (2002), *Radical Hollywood: The Untold Story Behind America's Favorite Movies* (New York: The New Press).

Ceplar, Larry and Steven Englund (1979), *The Inquisition in Hollywood: Politics in the Film Community, 1930–1960* (Berkeley: University of California Press).

Chandler, Charlotte (2002), *Nobody's Perfect: Billy Wilder – A Personal Biography* (New York: Applause Theatre & Cinema Books).

Chicago Tribune advertisement (1963), 1 December, Section 10, p. 11.

Cohan, Steven (2019), *Hollywood by Hollywood: The Backstudio Picture and the Mystique of Making Movies* (New York: Oxford University Press).

Colton, Helen (1949), 'No Wrinkles Grow on La Swanson: Glamorous Gloria Out to Vamp New Generation of Movie Fans as Faded Star Trying a Comeback in "Sunset Boulevard"', *New York Times*, 22 May, p. X5.

Crowe, Cameron (1999), *Conversations with Wilder* (New York: Knopf).

Desjardins, Mary (2010), 'An Appetite for Living: Gloria Swanson, Colleen Moore, and Clara Bow', in Patrice Petro (ed.), *Idols of Modernity: Movie Stars of the 1920s* (New Brunswick, NJ: Rutgers University Press), pp. 108–36.

Doherty, Thomas (2018), *Show Trial: Hollywood, HUAC, and the Birth of the Blacklist* (New York: Columbia University Press).

Fischer, Lucy (1988), '*Sunset Boulevard*: Fading Stars', in Janet Todd (ed.), *Women and Film*, New Series, vol. 4 (New York: Holmes & Meier), pp. 97–113.

Gautreau, Justin (2021), *The Last Word: The Hollywood Novel and the Studio System* (New York: Oxford University Press).

Gemünden, Gerd (2008), *A Foreign Affair: Billy Wilder's American Films* (New York: Berghahn Books).

Gladchuk, John Joseph (2007), *Hollywood and Anticommunism: HUAC and the Evolution of the Red Menace, 1935–1950* (New York: Routledge).

Grossman, Julie (2009), *Rethinking the Femme Fatale in Film Noir: Ready for Her Close-Up* (New York: Palgrave Macmillan).

Hirsch, Foster (1981), *Film Noir: The Dark Side of the Screen* (New York: Da Capo Press).
Hoffman, Leonard (1961), 'Gloria Swanson, on TV Next Friday, Can't Live Down that "Kookie" Role She Took on in "Sunset Boulevard"', *Chicago Tribune TV Week*, 9 December, pp. 8–9.
Joudrey, Tom (2020), 'Sunset Boulevard at 70: We're All Norma Desmond Now', *The Guardian* online, 4 August.
Koury, Phil (1948), 'The Happy Union of Brackett and Wilder: Unique Writer-Director, Writer-Producer Team Has Impressive Ten-Year Record', *New York Times*, 18 April, p. X5.
Lightman, Herb (1950), 'Old Master, New Tricks', *American Cinematographer*, September, pp. 309, 318, 320.
McBride, Joseph (2021), *Billy Wilder: Dancing on the Edge* (New York: Columbia University Press).
McBride, Joseph and Todd McCarthy (1979), 'Going for the Innings', *Film Comment* 15 (1), pp. 40–8.
McNally, Karen (2021), *The Stardom Film: Creating the Hollywood Fairy Tale* (New York: Wallflower).
Nadel, Alan (2018), *Demographic Angst: Cultural Narratives and American Films of the 1950s* (New Brunswick, NJ: Rutgers University Press).
Navasky, Victor S. ([1980] 1991), *Naming Names* (New York: Penguin).
Palmer, James (1985), '*In a Lonely Place*: Paranoia in the Dream Factory', *Literature/Film Quarterly* 13 (3), pp. 200–7.
Peberdy, Donna (2013), 'Acting and Performance in Film Noir', in Andrew Spicer and Helen Hanson (eds), *A Companion to Film Noir* (Chichester: Wiley Blackwell), pp. 318–34.
Perkins, V. S. (1992), '*In a Lonely Place*', in Ian Cameron (ed.), *The Book of Film Noir* (New York: Continuum), pp. 222–31.
Petro, Patrice (2010), 'Introduction: Stardom in the 1920s', in Patrice Petro (ed.), *Idols of Modernity: Movie Stars of the 1920s* (New Brunswick, NJ: Rutgers University Press), pp. 1–20.
Place, Janey (1998), 'Women in Film Noir', in E. Ann Kaplan (ed.), *Women in Film Noir* (London: British Film Institute), pp. 47–68.
Production Code Administration (1949), File on *Sunset Boulevard* in *Hollywood and the Production Code* (2006), filmed from the holdings of the Margaret Herrick Library, Woodbridge, CT.
Rich, Alan (1994), Review of *Swanson on Sunset*, *Variety*, 12–18 December, p. 88.
Schallert, Edwin (1950), '"Sunset Boulevard" Unique Sinister Hollywood Drama', *Los Angeles Times*, 25 August, p. 13.
Sikov, Ed (1998), *On Sunset Boulevard: The Life and Times of Billy Wilder* (New York: Hyperion).
Slide, Anthony (ed.) (2015), *'It's the Pictures That Got Small': Charles Brackett on Billy Wilder and Hollywood's Golden Age* (New York: Columbia University Press).

Staggs, Sam (2002), *Close-Up on Sunset Boulevard: Billy Wilder, Norma Desmond, and the Dark Hollywood Dream* (New York: St Martin's Griffin).

Sunset Boulevard (1956), [TV programme] NBC, 3 December.

'"Sunset" Looks to Music Hall Record' (1950), *Variety*, 13 September, p. 7.

Swanson, Gloria (1980), *Swanson on Swanson* (New York: Random House).

Taylor, Aaron (2007), 'Twilight of the Idols: Performance, Melodramatic Villainy, and *Sunset Boulevard*', *Journal of Film and Video* 5 (2), pp. 13–31.

Thomas, Bob (1983), *Golden Boy: The Untold Story of William Holden* (New York: St Martin's Press).

'Top-Grossers of 1950' (1951), *Variety*, 3 January, p. 58.

Trowbridge, Katelin (2002), 'The War Between Words and Images – *Sunset Boulevard*', *Literature/Film Quarterly* 30 (4), pp. 294–303.

Wilder, Billy (1999), *Sunset Boulevard* (Berkeley: University of California Press).

Wilder, Billy (2021), 'Stroheim, the Man We Love to Hate', in Noah Isenberg (ed.), *Billy Wilder on Assignment: Dispatches from Weimar Berlin and Interwar Vienna*, trans. Shelley Frisch (Princeton: Princeton University Press), pp. 148–52.

Zolotow, Maurice (1996), *Billy Wilder in Hollywood* (New York: Limelight Editions).